The World of
"Wood, Field,
and Stream"

The World of

Illustrated by John Groth

New York

Holt, Rinehart and Winston

"Wood, Field, and Stream"

*An Outdoorsman's Collection
from the columns
of the New York Times
by John W. Randolph*

Selected by Richard A. Wolters

With an Introduction by Red Smith

Introduction

Never in its rattling existence between assembly line and junk-pile did an automobile owned by Jack Randolph receive a bath. Jack steadfastly refused to clean or oil a shotgun, he considered window-washing pointless as long as light could filter through, and he ate dessert as the first course at dinner.

He was not more untidy or shiftless than most men; he simply had moral scruples against wasting on inanimate things the care and attention he believed should be reserved for living creatures, including people. He liked people and dogs. He also liked desserts and wanted to enjoy them while his appetite was keen. Ordering pie à la mode ahead of the soup got him some strange looks from waitresses, but he was a large man of impressive dignity and he usually won.

Jack was born in the country and is buried in the country, but most of the years between were spent on newspapers in cities. He did not believe that boyhood in a magnolia swamp gave him a key, denied to city folk, to unlock the mysteries of nature. Nature and life and death held as many mysteries for him as for anybody, though he was pretty sure he could name the ultimate destination of people who overcooked venison or beef.

The last and happiest of his many jobs was as outdoors editor of the New York *Times,* happiest for him and happiest for *Times* readers. He liked the outdoors, enjoyed fishing but preferred hunting. He did not regard himself as an expert in these matters and did not write expertise on the Fanwing Royal Coachman or the habits of upland birds.

Experts, of whom there are many among outdoors writers, made him uncomfortable. He would have throttled anyone who called him a nature-lover, would sooner have mixed strawberry pop with his bourbon than refer to nature as "She." He abhorred clichés and disliked the sort of person who habitually employs them, as you will discover reading his reference to "the man who says he has 'conquered' a mountain when he has crawled up the side of it."

"So," Jack wrote, "do ants conquer drainpipes."

I seem to go on about the things Jack Randolph wasn't and the way he didn't write when I should be saying what kind of man he was and how he did write. Well, he was big, generous, witty, independent, gentle, honest, gifted, thoughtful, original, kind and clearheaded, beloved in life and now widely mourned. He wrote like this:

"Vanity cost a nineteen-pound turkey gobbler his life today when a hunter caught him strutting in a field, sneaked up on him while he bragged on himself, and shot him dead."

I submit that it is not possible to write a better lead.

Thinking of Jack, I am reminded of Grantland Rice. After Granny's death in July, 1954, there was a party at Toots Shor's celebrating publication of his memoirs. It was November 1, Granny's birthday, and a raft of his friends like Jack Dempsey, Gene Sarazen, Douglas Fairbanks, Jr., and Johnny Weissmuller took part in a tribute to Granny on Ed Sullivan's television program. Toots had the show tuned in, but a noisy crowd at the bar made it difficult to catch. Rube Goldberg, at my side, must have seen me glance around in annoyance, for he spoke quietly.

"You know," he said, "if Granny were here he'd be back there at the bar. He was America's foremost enemy of blather."

I don't know whether Jack Randolph and Granny ever met, but they should have been great friends. They had so much in common.

—RED SMITH

Stamford, Conn.
October, 1961

vi

Contents

The World of
"Wood, Field,
and Stream"

Modern Hunter Only
Has to Look Stoic — Fancy
Equipment Does the Rest

Never has there been a time since men hunted with pointed sticks when the strong, hardy outdoorsman could be strong and hardy with so little inconvenience. The vast resources of modern technology are at the instant call of the modern gadget-master, whose equipment sees all, hears all, shelters all, warms and cools all, guides all, lures all, and, in theory, kills all.

Consider the modern deer hunter who rises from under his electric blanket in a centrally heated lodge to the chimes of an electric alarm clock, and begins the ceremony of dressing, which he often is able to do without help.

He dons his cotton-and-wool insulated underwear, and draws over that his insulated quilted underwear. His feet he clads in plastic insulated socks and either insulated rubber or insulated leather boots. His pants are not insulated, but they are made of fine wool with leather pockets and they cost enough to satisfy him, anyway.

His jacket is an architectural triumph of various layers, with rubber game-pockets, special pockets for shells (which he does

3

not need, since he also is wearing a special shell-belt), and a drop-flap that he may lower in order to sit dry on wet stumps. His cap is a lustrous yellow or red and it has ear-flaps, which he may need, although his jacket has a hood.

In the dining room, he lights four hand-warmers, two for his hand-pockets and two to stuff inside his shirt against his kidneys. He also fills a couple of cigarette-lighters. Into his pockets with these go a hand-compass, to use in case his wrist-compass goes wrong (his car-compass will guide him along the road) and a handful of fire-lighters in case he has to build a fire in the woods.

Around his neck he hangs a pair of powerful binoculars, to use when he doesn't care to lift his rifle in order to scan through its two-and-a-half- to eight-power compensating lenses.

It is time to put his ready-lunch into his game-pocket, along with a Thermos bottle of coffee (his full lunch will be in a thermal container in the car along with beer in a cooler and more hot coffee). Into the game-pocket with them may go his cushion, for sitting soft as well as dry.

Before stepping into the chill morning, he sprinkles deer-lure, made perhaps of apple essence, delicately on the lapel of his jacket, and puts his deer-call, made of plastic and a rubber band, into his pocket.

He now is almost ready to go sit down in the woods and wait for his guide to drive a deer his way. Of course, he takes his rifle, an auto-loader bearing the scope that does everything except cook the game.

He may want to take along a few other things, such as thermal gloves or mittens, a good mirror to enable him to see deer coming behind him, a pocket stove with canned fuel, a knife with blades on it for getting stones out of horses' hoofs, together with a German belt-knife for looks, a patent deer-pulling rope, a gun-cleaning kit in case he rams his rifle barrel trigger-deep into a swamp, and a silver flask full of whisky in case of faintness or freezing. And a bottle of chemical to keep fog off his spectacles, and a few vitamin pills.

But on the whole he is ready, prepared to stalk the woods with iron, impassive face, meeting all hardships like the stoic that he is. Hiawatha never had it so good.

Deer Tracks May Be Exciting, but They Cannot Be Hung in the Barn

Colrain, Massachusetts—Three or four inches of new snow are a great help to a deer hunter, especially when the snow keeps coming. It is a new page on which everything is written clearly.

So everybody saw deer tracks today; clear, new tracks. Clear, new tracks in fresh snow are a fine thing to look at, and very interesting to look at, and very exciting. But they are not deer, and cannot be hung in the barn. Fourteen anathemas on them.

Three of us started the day in just such snow by taking stands in the neighborhood of an old sugar house on Colrain Mountain. My own stand was against a great maple on the edge of an old field backed by thick pines in which deer love to hang around.

They were hanging around there, all right. Joe Jurek, who stood at the head of an old apple orchard a quarter of a mile away, had tired of cold feet when he put a good buck out of those pines a couple of hours later. But it didn't go past me, and it didn't go past Jurek's brother, Bill. It went over a little hardwood ridge, through a swamp, and over a pine ridge, and probably it is still going.

Somewhat later I had sense enough to move my frozen feet, and Bill Jurek elected to move his at the same time.

The three of us prowled that part of the mountain, which spread for miles, for several hours and saw plenty of fresh, clear, exciting deer tracks. Nobody caught sight of a flag.

There was shooting from every part of the compass, but none of it within a thousand yards of us. We met other hunters following fresh, clear tracks and did not shoot any of them. Others met us following fresh, clear tracks and did not shoot us. From this vital point of view, it was a successful day.

Late in the afternoon, when we had started toward the road,

we found where five deer had dawdled out through a sheep pasture, wandering aimlessly through the hardhack in plain sight for a quarter of a mile with nobody present to see them. Their course took them past several places where one or the other of us had stood or walked.

Less than twenty minutes after I had left that maple tree of freezing memory, a buck walked within thirty yards of it, with Lawrence Shearer, Jr., walking a few minutes behind it. He never caught up.

Another deer walked straight through Bill Jurek's former stand at about the same time.

The shooting went on all day long, and the Jureks and I listened to it with calm detachment. Strong, hardy outdoorsmen are never envious. They are just tired and half frozen.

Meanwhile, back at the ranch, three high-school seniors, all football players of local renown, set out to pit their inexperience against the cagey deer.

They are all eighteen years old and weigh in the neighborhood of two hundred pounds apiece, but they are only youths, after all. They could hardly be expected to outwit the trickiest game of the forest.

In time, as they garner the "Lore of the Wildwood," they may become journeymen deer hunters. But they are boys now, mere boys. They must observe, and learn.

They did not even hunt on Colrain Mountain but went to a nameless hill of no particular repute as a deer hangout, wandered to the top of it, sat down awhile, wandered about for a while, sat down again, and then went home. They went home with three deer. It was about noon.

But that is not the worst. A high-school *girl* killed her deer by 9:30 A.M. and was back in school before noon to receive the plaudits of the academic multitude. It was reported that she was overwhelmingly modest about the thing, but her classmates could think of nothing to do about it.

Two Dogs in a New England Kitchen Pose Problem for Philosophic Hunter

Colrain, Massachusetts—These two dogs moving around a New England kitchen illuminate the difference between Madison Avenue and the hunting field, but the trouble is that no solid conclusions can be seen clearly in the illumination.

There is Kelly, for example, more commonly known around here as Stupid. He was named for a Grace Kelly of Boston who is now Mrs. Paul Giorgioli of South Deerfield, Massachusetts. She is a professional dancer, perfectly named Grace, and he was therefore named Kelly because he was fat and clumsy as a puppy.

This Kelly dog is all personality, winsome, aristocratically clumsy, although he is a mongrel and useless.

His colleague and constant enemy is Mike, a beagle who was so named because the word Mike can be bellowed with some effect if he works. Mike is a fine gun dog, useful, efficient, industrious, enduring, and without very many social graces.

Stupid is large, black-and-white in the border collie manner, although his mother was a purebred springer, and elegantly languorous. He can sit awkwardly upright in a small upholstered chair in a way that makes women maudlin with admiration and affection, though they know he is fit for nothing beyond household pethood.

Mike, on the other hand, is small, muscular, black-and-white-and-brown, vigilant, and full of springy alertness that spells competence. Women rarely give him a second glance when Stupid is around and never want to hear what he can do with snowshoe rabbits.

What he can do with them is almost beyond belief. This short-legged dog, struggling and leaping through snow deeper than he is, can drive snowshoes all day long and has to be tolled off at nightfall by tricks and contrivances. Many and many a snowshoe and cottontail has been killed in front of him, but women don't care. Stupid's black, affectionate eyes fetch them.

If dogs were used for television commercials, as sooner or later they will be, Kelly would be the highest-priced jollyboy on earth, and I wish I owned him. Mike would never make the grade; he is strictly a production dog. He can produce rabbits, while Stupid hangs around the kitchen charming women.

There is something basic here—as they say on Madison Avenue—but what is it? Women, who do nine-tenths of the buying, are suckers for Stupid. But which dog should be more admired? Is money everything?

What about our good old American heritage, which says that a man or a boy should be able to go out and bring home game for the family pot any time he wants to? And doesn't everybody know that he can do that only with the help of a strong, keen-nosed, and faithful dog?

Are women going to sabotage and undermine this heritage by extravagant admiration for a big, clumsy, winsome, useless mutt that could not follow a rabbit a hundred yards but could easily sell billions of filters that both satisfy and build character, if hooked on to a show with a man who holds a cigarette straight up in the air while he interviews an idiot? This cannot be resolved, except by television. Mike will never get anywhere; he is only a fine rabbit dog who ain't never caught a rabbit but has driven many a one to the hunter. That Stupid is a character and could insult network vice-presidents if he wanted to.

Women Like to See Husbands
Go Fishing, Survey Shows,
but Reasons Differ

There is enough flapdoodle floating around in print about advice to the wives of fishermen, but nobody seems to feel that fishermen with wives need counsel.

As a matter of fact, they don't. They only seem to need it because of the general and mistaken belief that nonfishing women regard fishing with either amused tolerance or impatient contempt. If this were so, obviously, there would not be sixteen million anglers in this country, the vast majority of them males. Women are not that ineffectual.

A national survey just concluded by the actuarial division of the American Association for the Prevention of Uxoricide (est. April, 1957) has found that only one wife in 1,857 disputed her husband's right to fish and that only one in 943 thought her husband fished too much.

One New England woman was found who interdicted all fishing by her husband, would not let him use his car, forbade the ownership of any tackle, and sowed the backyard with quicklime to embargo worms.

But he was a man born to be bullied, and he fished regularly with the neighborhood children anyway. They let him use their tackle, carried him on their bike handlebars, and shared their lunches with him. In return, he umpired their ball games. He was seventy-four years old and didn't need dignity.

But this was a unique case. The A.A.P.U. actuaries, in interviews-in-depth with 63,814 wives, found that 82.64 per cent of them actively encouraged fishing by their husbands. Their motives, as disclosed by psychological analysis of interview transcriptions, were mainly these:

9

1. The wife likes her husband and thinks fishing is good for him.

2. The wife doesn't like her husband and is glad to be shut of him as often as possible.

3. The wife herself likes to fish.

Only 1.3 per cent thought fishing a sport for idiots, in spite of the fact that in all cases husbands had described at angry length the idiots that they met on streams and boats.

The vast majority, with cool female reasoning, held fishing to be simply a healthy sport. Their attitude was that it therefore did not rank with composing great music. But almost 20 per cent of them said they would rather see their husbands fishing without sideburns than doing bumps and grinds while singing about a houn' dog.

A trifle over 2.35 per cent were indifferent. Some of these did not know whether their husbands fished, just knew the men were often gone all day and that they always carried along some kind of long switch, some string, and something that looked like a pencil sharpener. These women, not classified by the psychologists as genius types, were put down in the "approve fishing" category because there was no other place to put them.

The wives who fished were the most difficult group; almost unclassifiable. Exactly 78 per cent felt that their husbands were clumsy fishermen but ought to keep trying. Just 12 per cent thought their husbands were so hopelessly inept that they ought to give it up. Just under 9 per cent regarded their husbands as anglers equal to the wives. More than 1 per cent admitted that their husbands could fish better than they. A little under 83 per cent of this 1 per cent-plus regarded their expert husbands as showboats and thought therefore that they ought to quit fishing or be psychoanalyzed.

This survey, and its overwhelming proof that wives either approve of or tolerate fishing, indicates to the unprejudiced eye that fishermen with wives are not in need of counsel. There is only one minor factor missing: the A.A.P.U. has been unable to find an unprejudiced eye.

Who Left the Tackle Box
on the Dock, Lost the Gaff,
and Broke the Rod?

Brielle, New Jersey—If there is anything a fishing trip needs, it is careful planning and vigilant attention to detail. The absent-minded angler is a pathetic figure, and two of them on one boat, as happened here, are too many.

It is not pleasant to have to tell this story, but it must be told for the good of fishing in general, though a couple of reputations may suffer.

R. W. (Bill) Schraeder of Point Pleasant, New Jersey, had scarcely run his fast cruiser *Explorer* a dozen miles from Brielle yesterday when it was discovered that neither of the tackle boxes belonging to Robert O'Byrne of New York was aboard.

I had taken them from the car, placed them on the dock beside the *Explorer,* and turned to other business. O'Byrne later muttered something about people not completing what they begin, but, of course, this was weak, weak. They were his tackle boxes, weren't they?

Well, we only had to run an extra twenty-five miles to go back for them, but it might have been costly.

Later, when Schraeder had brought a twenty-five-pound false albacore alongside, I gaffed it, taking care to get the point far back, so that the fish could be released. Schraeder had already said he wanted to release it. He freed the hook while I held the fish, and then said, "Throw him back."

It wasn't my fault that the short gaff was still in the false albacore when I obeyed the order. It was Schraeder's gaff, wasn't it, and wasn't it up to him to look out for it? Besides, it was his boat, and he was captain, and I had to obey his wishes for the sake of both seamanship and politeness.

Schraeder, now a realtor, used to be a commercial fisherman, and he should have known better. He admitted it, too; said he should have known better than to put his equipment in the hands of something or other, I didn't catch just what.

O'Byrne then couldn't find my streamer flies, with which he had intended to catch bonitos on a fly rod. He caught them anyway, on a strip of pork rind, but the lapse was painfully evident anyway. He denied that I had handed him those streamers earlier, and later it turned out that I hadn't, but only because he hadn't asked for them. He was the one who wanted to fish with streamers, and he had forgotten. Later, I found the streamers in my tackle bag, where they belong.

O'Byrne also caused me to knock the chum-spoon overboard and lose it, by calling my attention at the wrong moment to the fact that my line had snagged his. O'Byrne never watches that kind of thing; too busy thinking about his problems as sales director of the Sportsmen's Show in February.

He might have been thinking about that when he handed his bait rod and reel over to me to use. In any case, it was not my fault that a nut came off the reel handle and got lost. A man lending equipment should check it first. O'Byrne snarled something about the Black Plague. But irrelevant remarks never help.

It wasn't I, either, who stepped on the tip of his ultra-light spinning rod and broke it. I'm sure it was somebody else; it must have been.

It was Schraeder, though, who persuaded me to get my head up above the wind screen to see how fast the *Explorer* would go when he opened her up. With his experience, he ought to have known that the wind would snatch my long-billed cap and send it sailing. He just wasn't thinking.

That is the point: these men weren't thinking much. It takes thought and vigilance to run a fishing trip right.

Scientific Proof Now Available That "Diggety Wash" Salmon Can Be Hooked

St. Stephen, New Brunswick—The scientific proof is now available that salmon can be hooked in the Diggety Wash, or Digdeguash, as the illiterate mapmakers insist on spelling it.

Clinical evidence was obtained today by a field expedition, suitably equipped and led by Fred Brisley, renowned guide and fish research expert operating at Loon Bay Lodge on the St. Croix River. The party consisted of one strong, hardy outdoorsman who acted as research assistant, and the historian.

The proof was that in only twelve man-hours of fishing, one grilse, weighing seven or eight pounds, was hooked on a Blonde Wulff dry fly and almost instantly released. That was done by the research assistant.

Today's feat is a notable event in these parts, and it is expected that the Canadian Ministry of External Affairs will promptly and with suitable protocol inform the Spanish, Norwegian, Icelandic, United States, English, and Irish governments. All of these countries have interest in sports-fishing for salmon.

The little Diggety Wash, a tributary of the St. Croix, has had salmon for several years. Fish ascending the St. Croix and stopped by a dam at Callus, Maine (spelled Calais by the sloppy cartographers), turn back and ascend the smaller streams below the dam to spawn.

The Diggety Wash is one of these. The salmon are there, but almost nobody fishes for them, just as few anglers bother to fish the water below the dam at Callus, although there are salmon there, too. There was a scientific question whether the Diggety Wash salmon could be hooked.

It is true that Frank Flagg of St. Stephen caught two salmon there Tuesday, but that was not scientific: he had no historian.

The Diggety is a small stream, quite low and with only three or four pools in the region we fish. One of these is under a covered bridge and there are salmon visible in it. We passed that one up for a pool a couple of miles upstream that is not accessible by road.

Brisley, loyal to his scientific theory that these salmon were just like any other salmon, had fished the stream for six hours with me a few days ago. The next day Gordon Dean and Leo Mardin of New York, both expert salmon anglers, fished it for a good eight hours, with the help of George Welock, operator of Loon Bay Lodge. Nobody got a strike in these two days of work, yet Brisley was unconvinced.

He came pretty close to conviction today after we had fished for four hours in one pool in which salmon, big and small, leaped and rolled. None of them was taking lure.

Late in the day a fish began to feed at the edge of a ledge. His size and swirl made him look like a very big brown trout, and no salmon had been rising in that spot before. Brisley got a rise out of him with his surface stone fly and two rises with a light woolly worm, but the fish would not take.

I tried him with the Blonde Wulff, cast it perhaps fifteen feet into the middle of the stream to get some line out, and was about to retrieve for a full cast against the ledge when the fish rose and took it.

Now, of course, I could have caught that fish if I had wanted to, and I would have, too, if it had been a brown trout. But on his first leap, which carried him four or five feet in the air, I saw he was a salmon, so I let him shake the hook.

After all, we were there only to prove that salmon could be hooked there, and he had been hooked. Who wants to carry a heavy, wet, slippery fish through a half mile of brush and woods? It wouldn't have made sense to catch him.

Since the expedition mission had been accomplished, there didn't seem to be any point in fishing further, so after only two or three more hours of idle casting we packed up. Science had been served and the sum of human knowledge swelled.

14

How Farmer's Son Earned
His Hunting Boots: Heeded
Lesson, Didn't Shoot

Bernardston, Massachusetts—This is what happened today and what was said, and, if there is a moral in it, let a moralist find it.

A friend wearing a red shirt and I were hunting when we met a farmer and his son hunting. The farmer was a small man with a red, fiery face and with energy, independence, and positive opinion stamped all over him. We hunted along together for a while.

At one point my friend in the red shirt, walking on the far left as we went through a swampy meadow, entered a small patch of alders and was out of sight for a few seconds. During that time a cock pheasant rose in front of the farmer's son, who was a few yards to the right of the man in the alders.

The bird curved to the left but was still well in front of everybody when the boy lifted his gun. He didn't shoot. His father asked him why. "I couldn't see the man in the red shirt," the

15

boy snapped, and his face reddened in a way that proved whose son he was. "First good shot I had, too."

"Never mind that," his father said impatiently. "You done right and just won yourself that pair of hunting boots you been wanting. We'll quit early and go in town and make the buy."

That ended that. The boy killed a couple of birds later, but meanwhile he opened his gun at every fence, when we drew together to confer on our next move, and when we sat down for a smoke. He checked his safety every minute or so and watched the direction of the muzzle of his gun. He did everything right and safe.

Later I asked his father how he had taught the boy to observe safety rules so carefully.

"He was a pretty good boy to start with," the father said sharply, "and he wouldn't have been no fool if I hadn't told him a thing. But I done what I could to help.

"When he was twelve, I bought him a shotgun. It was against the law for him to hunt until he was sixteen, but I figured that at twelve he still thought I knew something, but at sixteen he'd think he knew everything. I only went to school to the sixth grade and he was already getting to know more than I did out of books. But it didn't turn out that way. He thinks he knows a heap, all right, but he listens. He'd better.

"Anyway, I took him out with his gun without shells and started teaching him how not to shoot people. Before I even let him load the gun, I had him so he'd open it to make sure it was empty when he even got in sight of a house. I'd even slip shells in it when he wasn't looking to see if he'd check and find them.

"When I was sure he was all right, I took him out on our own place, him hunting and me without a gun, and walked behind him and watched everything he done. I got a friend in town who was a gun expert and fine skeet shooter to come out and teach him to shoot and add some more safety stuff. Last year we hunted on our place, but I wouldn't let him hunt off it. The law is the law, and I don't aim to let anybody have nothing on me or any of my family.

"Well, Friday he got his first license and now it's up to him. I can't do no more, but that don't worry me none. He's all right now because he had the stuff to start with.

16

"He's a better shot than I am right now, but he don't know it yet. When he finds it out, that'll be the end of my influence and he'll probably start teaching me.

"Maybe that won't be a bad idea, if he can get me to listen like he did. This morning I was hunting alone while he was in school. A cock pheasant got up and I dropped it cold. It fell not more than ten feet from the nose of one of my own Jersey heifers. He don't know about that and I ain't going to tell him."

The little man's face hardened in sudden anger.

"But even if the boy finds out," he snapped, "he'll still listen to me and do what I say. There ain't but one boss around my house."

Skeet Shooter's Ability as Hunter Depends on His Score and His School of Logic

Bethany, Connecticut—An old argument is going on here, after a few rounds of skeet shooting: Can a good game shooter be a poor skeet shooter and vice versa?

It is an odd coincidence that the shooters who scored twenty-three or better maintain that a good shot was a good shot and could hit anything, game or target. The oafs who shot eleven to fourteen, however, argued with eloquence that plenty of good game shots couldn't hit a clay target.

The conventional argument is that the game shot needs something alive out in front of him to make him shoot well; something atavistic makes him center on the bird. Skeet shooters, the argument goes, never look so good in the field.

This position is maintained most fashionably by Richard Wolters of Ossining, who claims to have hit quail, pheasants, and ducks with marvelous facility. If the manufacturers would put feathers on clay targets, he would hit them every time. That is what he says. He said it several times while his score of thirteen was being counted.

People hanging around the Winchester Gun Club today listened to this silently. It is hard to know what a man is thinking on a skeet course when he works for a gun manufacturer, and most of these people work for Olin Mathieson. They all rate as pros and are obliged to be crack shots. Their wives, many of whom are here, rate as associate pros or proconsorts and must shoot twenty or better to stay out of the divorce courts.

It should be reported immediately, for the sake of his job, that Scott Healy of Winchester shot a twenty-three. The hang-dog look he assumed after the round was mere grandstanding. His wife Nancy shot a twenty and looked better doing it. They will still be married next month.

Watching Ken Janson was a disagreeable experience. He was shooting a modest seventeen last summer. He shot twenty-four today, powdering birds almost before they left the trap. A man can lose friends that way. But Janson is Winchester's research chief and he is bound to be a shark.

Let us say nothing of what Gene Brown and Jim Rikhoff did. It is an ill thing to blow the whistle on a man's job. And they might not have been feeling well anyway.

These twenty-and-up scores are all very well for people who want to sell guns and ammunition, but are they worth the trouble? I could have shot twenty-three or so myself if I had wanted to compete, but I was trying a new system. It didn't seem worthwhile to go around grandstanding.

Besides, I agree that good skeet shots are not good game shots. A hunter has to be careful not to upset his game eye by dawdling around too much with these clay playthings. How can he know that he might not miss a grouse next fall because of hitting too many targets this summer?

With Wolters, it is only an excuse for missing targets, but the thing can be a serious, logical reason. Brown says it is a serious, logical reason with him. He had to keep talking anyway; he followed Nancy Healy on the course and was followed by Janson.

Wolters prefers not to talk about what his wife Olive shot, and she was using a .410 while he was using a 12. Furthermore, it was a new gun and she had shot skeet only once before. Mrs.

Wolters didn't mean to make him look bad. She was shooting in another group and didn't realize what she was doing.

It was an encouraging day. I know now that I am going to hit game on every shot next fall.

Don't Waste Time
Studying Woodcraft: Brush Up
on Machiavelli Instead

There has been a great deal of discussion lately in literary haunts and joints about what a sportsman should take along with him to read in hunting or fishing lodges, hotels, and camps.

It is possible to make a fairly exact list. The list is immediately limited by the fact that most of these places already have a great deal of reading material around, most of it concerning hunting and fishing. But there is no advantage for a sportsman in reading what his companions are reading; he has got to have private material for his monologues. Without it, he can hold the floor by persistent roaring, but he cannot astound or impress.

Furthermore, he must be alert to improve his technique as well as increase his material. A man can dominate a conversation by sheer will; with good technique he can overwhelm it. So his reading must all be useful.

Critics and commentators have worked out a reading list that is compact for travel, comprehensive, classical, and guaranteed to enable any hunter or fisherman to talk for hours with authority. It includes no hunting or fishing how-to-do-it stuff, which is dangerous material among strong, hardy outdoorsmen. Here is the list:

Any thick book on economics, old or new. A recent one might be better, since the musical jargon of economics changes from year to year and a word this year might not have the same meaning this year that it didn't have last year. The great advantage of this material is that it cannot be contradicted, any more than a fog can be resisted. Good, strong, technical stuff about the behavior of money and goods can resist any attempt to interrupt and may induce sleep. It is especially effective if bankers or corporation presidents are around.

One chapter of Machiavelli, "On How a Prince Should Keep Faith." This is for instruction in technique. Too many hunters practice lying and dissembling with no other purpose than deception or to hear themselves talk. Nobody can lie or dissemble properly about hunting and fishing without some purpose, such as to prove that he has some quality that he fancies his companions will admire. They never do, but he should have an aim. Machiavelli, in showing him that a smart prince never welshes on a deal just for the fun of it, will lead him gently to sound, effective fishing and hunting lies.

A World War I copy of the *Infantry Drill Regulation,* if he has had no military service. It will help him to talk intelligently to ex-servicemen and even to shout them down. They never read it.

The second volume of *The Decline and Fall of the Roman Empire,* if he has not read the first volume. Gibbon assumed that his readers already knew the facts and chronology of history intimately and could read Latin and Greek. Plunging into the middle of this book will help him to interrupt and take charge of discussions already in progress.

Any heavy catalogue on the gear of hunting or fishing, whichever he may be doing at the time. It will help him to prove that all of his companions are carrying the wrong tackle, guns, and clothing.

A cookbook or treatise on gastronomy, or both, the less well known the better. This is important, even vital. Without it, only a true gourmet can criticize the cooking in detail, suggest menus to the hotel or lodge operator, instruct his companions in the preparation and savoring of food, and make himself generally useful in a dietary way. A month or so ago I saw Charles Blake of Braintree, Massachusetts, completely rout a hunter who tried to do these things without first boning up. This man talked loudly and without preparation about food for some time before fixing Blake with a beady eye and demanding:

"Do you know the correct way to cook deer liver?"

"Yes, I know the correct way to cook deer liver," Charles Blake of Braintree, Massachusetts, snarled. "You throw it in a blasted skillet, fry it, and eat it. That's the correct way to cook deer liver."

He might not have said blasted; might have used some other word. But the ring of authority was there. He had studied the thing.

A sportsman doesn't need any more than that, except a loud voice and a strong will. These books will give him all the material and guidance he needs.

Naturally, he will take along his regular reading. On a rainy day there is nothing like curling up in a window seat with a good comic book.

Fishing Fortune Strikes Discordant Note as Angler's Fourteen-Year Sail Quest Ends

Anglers are not born, they are made by circumstances, and sometimes it takes a long time to get the right circumstances together. The bits of jigsaw have now fitted together for Mrs. Joan Loubet and it is already plain that her case is hopeless.

Mrs. Loubet is the wife of Nat Loubet, managing editor of *Ring* magazine, and daughter of Nat Fleischer, its publisher. She is said to have cut her baby teeth on a miniature ring-post and to have mastered baseball box scores before she could read Goldilocks.

But fishing was not her pidgin. Her husband will not say, possibly out of respect to his father-in-law, that he likes fishing better than boxing, but the record book says that, when March began, he had been trying to catch a sailfish for fourteen years.

During that period, he had fished the Florida coast, Haiti, the

Virgin Islands, Jamaica, and other West Indian areas and had caught fish of one kind or another, including tarpon and blue marlin. But he had never taken a sail. Never even had a strike.

During the last couple of years, Mrs. Loubet has been going along on some of his fishing trips, but strictly for laughs. The circumstances were not yet right.

Then fortune, or disaster, struck. The Loubets were fishing recently out of Marathon, Florida, with Captain Budd Carr, and Loubet, as usual, was trying wearily to get a sail. He had about given up, but inertia kept him from stopping.

Loubet had fished for four hours with no luck and was dispiritedly eating a sandwich and drinking a beer. A sail struck and he lost the beer overboard. He did not know until he had landed the sail twenty minutes later that the sandwich was still gripped in his teeth. It was a small sail, five feet eight inches long.

Mrs. Loubet was pleased, in a wifely sort of way: the poor guy had been trying so long. She said so, and at that point a sailfish hit her bait, plucking her from the chair. Mrs. Loubet is five feet tall and weighs one hundred pounds carrying a dictionary. She was headed over the boat's transom when Loubet and Carr grabbed her.

They put her back in the chair, strapped her down, and in the course of the next half hour she brought a sail to gaff. It was seven feet long.

Loubet was brooding over the injustice of fate next morning when his wife, already dressed for fishing and wearing suntan oil, demanded to know how much good fishing time he was going to waste sitting around over coffee. She wanted to know what they were down there for, anyway. She said, to a man who had tried to catch a sailfish for fourteen years, that you couldn't catch a sailfish without getting out there on the water.

Loubet has recovered, to some extent. He has caught his sailfish, however small, and the gnawings of frustration are assuaged. But the man is uneasy, full of vague forebodings. He is married to a fierce angler, to whom fishing is no longer a laughing matter, and Loubet is worrying about how he is going to find the time to do all the fishing he will have to do from here on out.

22

Table of Weights Is Blow
to Deer Hunter, but He Has
Several Honest Ways Out

It is a dirty trick to assemble and make public a table by which a deerslayer may determine the live weight of a deer he has slain simply by looking it up opposite the dressed weight in the table. But the thing has been done now, and nothing can diminish the harm that is bound to ensue.

Hunters have little enough imagination and invention to adorn their poor stories about the wildwood, though they are not quite so mentally torpid as fishermen. This sneaky table robs them of one of the best of their threadbare resources: the right to overestimate honestly the live weight of any deer they may accidentally kill.

It is odd that the blow should be delivered by Winchester Arms, which depends largely upon hunters for its existence. How can Winchester hope to sell arms and ammunition by lowgrading the prizes of its customers?

The table, published in *Winchester Proof,* a publicity sheet, nails the deer hunter to a cross of paper. If it is correct, and it almost certainly is, the deerslayer will know without doubt that the fawn that he had downed and that weighs 60 pounds dressed weighed only 80 pounds when it was alive.

Without the incriminating table, he could honestly guess that live weight as maybe 110, 115, and thereby promote his prize from fawn to young adult. But he cannot do this honestly now, and every red-blooded American outdoorsman considers himself a man of rugged honesty.

There is no use trying to cover the matter up, or slur it over. A fawn that weighs forty pounds dressed weighed fifty-five alive. These are the dressed weights followed by the live weights: 50–65, 70–90, 80–105, 90–115, 100–130, 110–140, 120–155,

23

130–165, 140–180, 150–190, 160–205, 170–215, 180–230, 190–240, 200–255, and 210–265.

This leaves little hope for the average hunter except the brassy lie, which is the most valued resource of the trained operator but a dangerous boomerang in the hands of the witless. Average hunters either bluster or cringe when attempting to use it.

But one hope is left. A man with the right kind of memory can throw the table away and remember only that there is a difference of 55 pounds between the dressed and live weight of a deer, forgetting as immaterial that this applies only to a deer that weighs 200 pounds dressed. By applying this to the scrawny 50-pounder he can arrive at a respectable 105 pounds.

He can reverse this, too. Since a deer weighing 60 pounds dressed weighed 80 alive, it is plain that by adding a third to the dressed weight he can arrive at the real live weight. Therefore, his big 210-pounder weighed 280 alive, instead of 265, and he can honestly say that he slew a 280-pound deer.

The important thing is to get rid of the table. Why should anybody let Winchester make him carry an anvil around on his back?

Young Goat Dressed as an Illegal Doe Deceives Two Hunters' Wives

A couple of western Massachusetts deer hunters have been in a dilemma for a couple of years over what their attitude should be toward the game laws. They have concluded that every decent hunter should obey every law, but that he is not obliged to brag about it or even to make claims that he obeys.

Their wives were the subversive influences. These two men, whose names were not Smith and Jones, had hunted bucks in

Vermont for a week without getting a shot. Every evening they endured torrents of contempt from their wives, who love venison.

At the end of the seventh shotless day they were returning home when Smith, a cow trader, stopped to see a farmer and found him taking down the carcass of a young goat, which had hung for a week. It struck Smith and Jones that a goat with its lower legs cut off looked much like a young deer.

They bought the goat, took it to Smith's home, where both women were waiting, hung it in the garage, and announced that they had killed a deer. But they said Smith had shot it by mistake; it was a small, illegal doe. They said they had been afraid to report it but hadn't wanted to leave it in the woods, so had brought it home illegally.

Women as a whole probably cannot be classified as criminals, but they are never so happy as when they have run a red light without getting caught. These women were enchanted. They had venison, and quickly brushed aside legal questions as irrelevant and incompetent.

Small steaks were quickly carved from the goat, broiled, and eaten on the spot.

"Oh, divine!" Mrs. Smith trilled. "The best venison I ever tasted!"

"Not too much wild taste!" Mrs. Jones exulted. "Just exactly the right amount!"

Both families ate from that goat for a month, off and on, and both wives were delighted. Smith and Jones, though, of course, they could not be heroes to their wives, were cordially tolerated for as much as a week.

Nobody ever questioned that the goat was venison and nobody ever mentioned any laws.

The following October, Jones went pheasant hunting with a friend and told him the story, swearing him to secrecy. But the friend came to dinner that night, drank several milk shakes, and could not hold his tongue. He spilled it.

Jones, struck dumb by terror, awaited the blow. But it did not fall. His wife reacted with inexplicable serenity, laughing mildly and playing the gracious hostess with determined charm. It was only when the friend left that Jones got his explanation. His wife began immediately to laugh ungovernably.

"It was all I could do not to laugh in his face," she shrieked. "I knew you had told him the story so he couldn't spread it around that you and Louis had shot a doe in Vermont. And, golly, he *believed* it!"

But that is not the end. Somebody else told them the goat story and they did believe it. Smith and Jones were reminded angrily for months that they were phonies. And Mrs. Smith and Mrs. Jones didn't want to hear anything about laws. They still don't.

Moral: Obey the hunting laws and keep your mouth shut.

Fate of Nineteen-Pound Turkey in Alabama Proves Pride Goeth Before a Fall

Claiborne, Alabama—Vanity cost a nineteen-pound turkey gobbler his life today when a hunter caught him strutting in a field, sneaked up on him while he bragged on himself, and shot him dead.

The general feeling among the fanatical turkey hunters of South Alabama is that nobody can sneak up on a wild gobbler unless he is strutting; at all other times he is too scary.

A turkey is strutting when he swells up, fans his tail, and stomps around dragging his wings and gobbling. Self-esteem is working in him so powerfully that he is about ready to take over a television variety show of his own and insult network vice-presidents. He is oblivious of everything on earth except himself.

The theory is that gobblers do this to make hens admire them, but this is plainly flapdoodle; turkeys hens can't be that silly. Turkeys strut for the same reason that men make long speeches.

Robert Hornung of Mobile located this gobbler big-wheeling in the middle of a wide field not far from the Alabama River.

Hornung, an unbreakably addicted turkey hunter who was acting as a volunteer hunter, spotted the gobbler with binoculars.

There was nothing much to it after that. He simply conducted his companion to the edge of the field and crawled with him to within shotgun range of the gobbler. His hunter, the Reverend T. M. Cullen of Ireland and Mobile, then killed it with a single blast.

It was not difficult for the fireside philosophers at the Claiborne Hunting Club, refreshing themselves with healthful milk shakes later, to decide gravely that this event had proved that pride goeth before a fall.

The philosophers needed nothing of the sort to replenish their faith in the laws of nature. For several days nobody had been able to call up a turkey, or even get an answer to yelping, or yepping, with mouth-calls and cedar-and-slate calls. It seemed that there were no wild turkeys left on the club territory.

This would be hard to believe, but human faith is easily shaken. The club has thirteen thousand acres of hunting land, some say sixteen thousand, and flocks of haughty turkeys are sometimes seen feeding in the open on some of those acres. But hunters, leaving the big cedar-log clubhouse about nine miles into the woods from a paved road, had had no sight or sound of them until the strutter bit the dust today.

An hour or so later, four hunters who were returning to the club on foot after leaving another car stuck in a mud hole flushed about fifteen from brush beside the eroded dirt road. All guns had been left in the car, which was pulled out later and driven to the club.

It is not possible to report that philosophy triumphed over emotion at that point. It is said that strong statements were made. I was not there and cannot support the charge.

At the moment I was making strong statements elsewhere in the vicinity. Clarence Dixon of Mobile and I were walking approximately thirty-seven miles, though Dixon cautiously estimated it was only seven, through low woods and over ridges, stopping here and there at likely places to try our yelpers. No answers.

At odd moments we and others whiled away the time jacking up cars stuck in mud holes and wedging rocks and logs under the wheels for traction. This is largely futile, but it exercises muscles, ingenuity, and vocabulary. In the end somebody can always be sent for Jason Fancie, the camp cook, whose cabin is near the club, and his pair of mules. This is never futile; no car is stuck in the mud at this moment.

The philosophers are tired now. Many of them won new honors today carrying what they call horse-head rocks to mud holes. But they are encouraged, and faith is reviving. A man might catch a gobbler any time.

This Tale Shows That
to Lure Salmon You Have
to Think Like One

In recent months, several letters have asked how trout and salmon flies are invented. The general answer is, of course, that nobody knows, except the inventors, who ordinarily are willing to tell but usually are incoherent.

Still, there are general principles. Flies usually are designed either to copy some insect as nearly as possible or just to attract the attention of fish. They are invented by (1) people trying to think like Einstein, (2) people trying to think like fish, or (3) people trying not to think.

According to twenty-year records kept by the actuarial division of the information department of the Sociedad de Pescadores Internacionales at its world headquarters in Geneva, these three groups are about equally successful, with the edge going to the nonthinkers. The nonthinker simply ties hackle, wool, tinsel, and stuff together in a way that suits his vacant fancy.

However, there is a detailed case at hand fitting into the category of people who try to think like fish. It has the virtues of being new, successful, and specific.

This is a salmon fly designed within the last month and used on the Mirimichi in New Brunswick. It caught many salmon. Nobody, including the man who designed it, knows why.

Jim Deren, the proprietor of the Anglers Roost in the Chrysler Building, is a man who is strong but not particularly silent. He tells the story of this nonpareil.

Deren, fishing with Al Marlon and Dan White of Brooklyn, Dr. Ralph Frimmer of White Plains, and Al and Bud Glen of Milwaukee, at O'Haire's Camp, Blacksville, New Brunswick, noticed three points in common among the nameless local flies that were taking salmon.

All of them had orange and black wool bodies, all had red squirrel-tail wings, and all had gold oval tinsel on the bodies. Deren dressed a composite, with black and orange wool bodies, red wings, and oval gold tinsel wrapped from tail to head, back to tail, and back to head again. This produced a gold-diamond pattern.

All of the party used that fly, which Deren called the Harlequin, and all caught fish. Deren caught and released eight salmon the first day. He netted three weighing more than twenty pounds (Deren kills no fish and this is an estimate). It is true that the Mirimichi fishing just before the season closed October 1 was terrific, but the fly was still a good bet—at that time anyway.

Why would these Mirimichi salmon like a gold-diamond body pattern on a Number 8 hook? Nobody knows, except the Mirimichi salmon, and maybe Deren, who says he was trying to think like one. He says to think like a salmon, you have to bug your eyes, open your mouth, and try to look like a salmon. Such a serious researcher scarcely can expect to attract fish and women simultaneously.

Hunters and Anglers With Real "Class" Must Be Languid, Above All Else

Colrain, Massachusetts—One of the unnoticed arts that the strong, hardy American outdoorsman has developed to a high degree in the last few years is the art of sitting down. He has done it by his own perserverance, with the vigilant help of American free enterprise.

It is no longer enough for an angler to sit on a boat thwart, even with a cushion on it, or for the hunter to sit on a stump; there is no class in it, and no indication of either progress or status. But he doesn't have to do it anyway. American free enterprise has thought up all kinds of sporting seats.

A couple of weeks ago I fished for shad in a boat on the Connecticut River a few feet from another boat in which an expert shad angler was taking fish every minute or so. But he wasn't just catching shad; he was doing it with a languid dash that made him seem to have a silk scarf around his throat, though there was nothing on his throat but an Adam's apple.

This angler was seated in an aluminum-and-canvas reclining lawn chair, with his feet propped up on a pillow in the bow of the boat. He didn't even unprop them when he hooked into a fish; just sat on the back of his neck, played the fish, and reached lazily for the net when the fish was close to the boat. This was gracious living.

A couple of years ago a manufacturer thought up the Hot Seat, a red pillow made of some kind of slick stuff with something inside it. It is for deer hunters, mainly. When the hunter sits on it, the thing warms up. It is wonderful, though a little unhandy to carry around. I have tried it and sat in the woods as comfortably as a Madison Avenue ninny on the back of a white horse in a photographer's studio.

30

Now comes the Old Pal, product of the Animal Trap Company of America at Lititz, Pennsylvania. This is for both hunting and fishing, for watching races from a concrete lawn or Little League games from behind the backstop, or auctions in a barnyard.

This little stool is made of tubing, so cunningly contrived that it folds together, and a little strip of red canvas. A fisherman can put it in anything from a dugout on up, and a hunter can carry it easily along with his gun, two compasses, lunch and Thermos bottles, first-aid kit, trick knives, rain jacket, extra sweater, pocket-warmers, fire-lighters, dry socks, and other minimum requirements of his Spartan sport.

I thought a couple of days ago that we might be moving backwards, retrogressing toward the animal state. Lawton Carver said the best thing he ever sat on while fishing was a short section of hickory stump placed in the bow of a double-ender on a Mississippi blackwater creek, and he wished he could do it again.

This worried me seriously for a minute; it was a sign of reaction and revolt against progress. But then things cleared up: Carver was sitting on a comfortable bar stool in his Second Avenue saloon, and he wasn't about to move. A hickory stump might look all right to him if it had foam rubber on it. Besides, he is a fly fisherman and has to stand up to fish.

Final and total reassurance came yesterday when I met a barefoot boy fishing the Deerfield River near Greenfield. Well, he was almost barefoot; wore nothing but sneakers on his feet, and in addition nothing but bathing trunks, a striped sport shirt, an expensive-looking tackle pack, and a cap bearing a yacht-club patch. He was coming out of the river to rest.

Before he sat down to rest, he went up the bank to his sports roadster, drew from it an object, brought it back to a shady place, and inflated it by lung power. Then he sat down on it.

Woman on First Deer-Hunting
Trip Stops Reading Long
Enough to Shoot Buck

Loon Bay, New Brunswick—A woman from Loon Bay Lodge slew a deer today under extraordinary circumstances, even for a woman.

All ended well, but two professional guides, neither of them known to be excitable, were shaken by the whole business.

The woman was tastefully attired in scarlet hunting pants and shirt, which she said belonged to her nineteen-year-old son, a college freshman fullback measuring six feet two inches and weighing a hundred and ninety-six pounds. Over the shirt she wore a zippered waterproof hunting jacket, and over all she wore a rain suit of overalls and jacket.

On her head a scarlet deer-stalker cap, with bill in front and back and ear-flaps tied on top, rested gracefully.

Her guide, Beecher Scott, took all this with remarkable aplomb. He led her to a birch ridge near the St. Croix River, chose a strategic spot for her, and invited her to sit. This she did upon something called a Hot Seat, given to her by Bud Leavitt of the Bangor, Maine, *Daily News.* It is a scarlet cushion containing a chemical that causes it to become warm when sat upon.

Ten minutes later this woman was well settled and living it up in the Canadian woods. Her cigarette was going fine. She was reading *The Wapshot Chronicle,* by John Cheever, and later she allowed it was pretty good. It had been raining for two days and the book got a little wet, but it wasn't hers anyway.

It might have been half an hour later when she looked up casually from this chronicle of a New England family and noticed that a small doe was standing a few feet away looking at her curiously. The sight interested her, and presently it occurred to her that across her lap lay a Winchester Model 88 lever-action rifle of .243 caliber. It was loaded.

The doe stood still while she aimed and clicked the trigger. It stood still while she worked the lever and jacked a shell into the chamber. It stood still while she aimed, but it jumped when she fired and dropped a small buck standing a few feet behind and to one side of the doe. The shooter had not seen the buck.

Warming to this fascinating business, she fired four rapid shots at the doe as it bounded off through the birches. There is no evidence that she hit the doe. Later it developed that the buck had been the victim of a spectacular shot. A sliver of lead had entered its right ear and hit the brain. Apparently the bullet had first struck a birch and split apart, one part hitting the buck.

The woman returned contentedly to her book. A little later Scott and my guide, Fred Brisley, came up and dressed out the deer. She greeted them cordially and turned another page of *The Wapshot Chronicle.* She had never hunted deer before and didn't see anything difficult enough about it to bring on hysterics.

This "Rogues' Gallery"
Describes Men Certain
to Ruin Hunting Trips

The subject of what kind of people to hunt with came up a few days ago, just about the time that all strong, hardy outdoorsmen began to grind their teeth about how many ducks, grouse, deer, and things they were going to kill this year.

It is an important subject right now, and the outdoorsmen around Gough's Indoor Campfire Circle on Forty-third Street were giving it grave attention. The consensus, after things quieted down, was that it was more important to know whom not to hunt with.

Safety considerations were put aside. All agreed that it was nice not to get killed in the woods. A few well-drawn categories of hunters-not-to-hunt-with emerged, and all agreed upon them, as well as any two or more men can agree in that particular forum.

The most detestable of these, of course, is the Nature-Lover. Nobody wants to hunt with him because he doesn't want to hunt. He wants to love nature. He will get in everybody's way loving it all over the landscape. This sort of hunter should have been a crooner.

The Home-Lover: Two hours after starting to hunt, he wants to go home. Just remembered that he promised his wife to fix the cellar door. Or is expecting a long-distance call. Or his ankle hurts. This always happens when he has not had a shot. Almost always when the party is using only one car—his.

The Thinker: Named for Rodin's famous work that was not named "The Thinker." He just loves to rest and will drop to the ground when anybody else stops to light a cigarette or tighten a shoelace. Spends most of his day sitting and exhausts his companions, whose efforts to get him up merely amuse him. This type can be tolerated in deer hunting, but not in upland game hunting. He is a cousin of the Home-Lover.

The Shot-Hog: He will be the first behind the dogs on every point. He always grabs the best stand in deer hunting if there is a drive on. Always tries to get the best position if dogs are running rabbits and will cut across a rabbit's running circle to intercept it ahead of somebody else.

If two men fire and drop a bird or deer or rabbit or duck, he always will yell, "I got him!" Then he will pick up the game, even if the bird has started to fall or the rabbit to roll before he fires. Never offers to divide game with companion who has killed little or nothing.

The Shell Pauper: Always discovers, after arriving at hunting cover ten miles or more from any store, that he is short of shells. Borrows, never to repay.

The Natural Leader: In some ways, he is even worse than the Nature-Lover. Organizes and directs everything. Tells everybody where to stand for deer or how to approach dogs on point. Decides when territory is exhausted and selects new territory. Decides who is to ride in which car. Rarely has a car of his own. Makes instant rulings on everything. Oddly enough, is rarely a Game Hog. Wants everybody to get game, but takes full credit for all successes.

The Purist: He knows the correct way to do everything and knows that all other ways are inadmissible. Tells everybody how they have slipped up in training their dogs, and knows the only brand of dog food that will keep a dog healthy. Insists on a tiny, Indian-like fire at noontime, when everybody else wants a big warm one. Has the only correct rifle or shotgun, boots, hunting coat, and knife. Shoots the only correct load. Should have been a butler.

The Babbler: Spends the whole of every hunting trip describing former hunting trips in which he, but nobody else present, participated. Should have been a woman.

Well, there are other kindred types, and I don't want to hear about them. Thinking about these has been too much for me. I should have been a hermit.

Posted Fishing Areas
Are Usually Challenge
to Spirited, Restless Schoolboys

Colrain, Massachusetts—There is not much posted water in this immediate region, but there is enough to keep the schoolboys happy.

The public water is fairly plentiful, all the way from the famous Deerfield River, in which fine brown trout are said to abound, to remote brooks, and the fishing pressure is not great. On a fair day, a reasonably skillful angler can take trout in a stream open to anybody.

But that sort of thing eventually palls on a boy. If there is no *verboten* water within striking distance, he is likely to get restless and maybe start hot-rodding or matching nickels.

When I was a boy, I lived in a part of the country where there is no posted land, and because of that I might easily have become a pool-hall character. But I never could learn to shoot a good stick. I had to pretend that all fishing was against the law, and there is no telling what damage this paltry sham works on the character.

There are just about enough posted brooks in the Colrain area for juvenile purposes. A few less and the pressure on them would be too much. As it is, they are fished hardly more than the public water.

One man here watches his posted water with binoculars from his barn. Of course, the boys fish it right under the glasses. They don't mind getting wet and muddy and scratched through the bushes. They'd rather do it than bank the nine-ball into the side pocket. And the owner is presumably happy hoarding his brook.

Another posts a brook that runs along a state road. His signs carry an extra legend saying, "THIS BROOK IS STOCKED BY THE

OWNER." He is evidently a man of vaulting courage, fit to challenge the most powerful forces of human nature.

The boys fish his brook, mostly at night, but the more spirited natures fish it by day. One boy waits until the owner himself is fishing, locates him, and then actually fishes the brook ahead of him. In local grammar-school circles this is regarded as a piece of virtuosity.

Some day a landowner is going to advertise that boys under sixteen may fish his posted land as much as they like. It will be a stroke of genius. It will be far better than a typhoid warning. A self-respecting boy caught fishing that water would die of shame.

A Dim View of Outdoor Glasses: Keep a Plentiful Supply Handy

So long as there is never going to be any real fishing this summer, or any summer either, a strong, hardy outdoorsman might as well sit down and figure out what kind of outdoor glasses he is going to buy next.

He is certainly going to buy more of some kind, since nothing makes a man feel so well equipped to catch fish or shoot game as enough outdoor glasses.

As a general proposition, ten or twelve pairs ought to get a man by, in addition to the regular glasses he wears for reading, working, and snarling at television commercials. The outdoorsman with twenty-twenty vision probably can get along with a half dozen.

The trouble is that attrition is high.

Consider the case of Polaroid dark glasses. These are valuable in fresh-water fishing and essential for glaring salt water, if the angler wants to see fish beneath the surface. But what kind?

Ground-to-prescription Polaroids are wonderful, if the right frames can be obtained. The trouble is that they are always left on boats, usually on map shelves. This is not because of absent-mindedness or general bat-headedness, but simply because prescription Polaroids are always left on map shelves. This can get to be expensive.

One alternative is the clip-on, which carries little wire gidgeons to slide over the top of the regular glasses. The plastic clip-ons are as light as a thought in a barroom, for a while. But after an hour or so, small anvils tend to become attached to them, and the bridge of the nose becomes a gully. And after a couple of days of fishing they acquire scratches and abrasions, always directly in front of the pupil, so that a small seagull is always sailing steadily in front of each eye.

Glass clip-ons are too heavy to begin with.

Either glass or plastic Polaroids with their own frames and ear-pieces that are worn over the regular glasses are pretty good, too, but they are unsteady and a good wind is likely to snatch them off.

The same applies to clear non-Polaroid, non-prescription glasses, either plastic or glass. Too heavy, too unsteady, or too scratched and abraded.

The solution lies in numbers. A well-equipped outdoorsman always has outdoor glasses stowed away in jackets, tackle vests, tackle boxes, car glove compartments, and everywhere else except in plain sight at home. Glasses left in sight at home will always be picked up by the careful housewife and carefully laid away under four layers of useless clothing in a cedar chest. There is no exception to this rule.

The big yellow hunting glasses, or "haze-cutters," are wonderful, too, for hunting on dark or bright days and for night-driving. But the frames are invariably so slight and insecure that a step into a stump-hole sends them flying eight or ten feet, always against a rock. My prescription pair is bulletproof, I think; they are thick enough for window glass on Trujillo's limousine, and heavy enough.

I did have good, heavy, secure frames for these, but somebody, I forget who, left them on top of a space-heater in a

Florida motel and the frames melted. They were the last pair of such frames in existence, of course.

Well, it's time to get another pair of something.

These, I think, will be glass Polaroids with tire tape extending from ear-frame to ear-frame under the chin and over the top of the head. But it's no use. Somebody will leave them on a stove.

Companions Are Prepared
for All Trouble Except What
Our Man Put His Foot Into

Loon Bay, New Brunswick—Norman H. Burg and Arthur Raphael of New York left Loon Bay Lodge this morning full of confidence, though it was raining hard and the woods were wet. They were confident because each of them possessed:

A poncho, a messkit, a haversack, an axe, a hatchet, a hunting knife, a compass (Burg had three of them, including a wrist-compass), an air mattress, a sleeping bag, a knapsack to carry the duffle bag, and boots of various kinds.

They were not carrying all this equipment, but they were carrying most of it.

Burg and Raphael came back full of bounce and determined to change rifles tomorrow. They have five rifles between them and maybe one of them will find a deer tomorrow. But they are not going to carry their seven-and-a-half horsepower outboard motor.

Meanwhile, back in the woods, Fred Brisley, my guide, and I were traipsing over various logging roads and through wet brush to no particular purpose. Neither of us could even find any fresh deer sign. It made me wish I had some of Burg's water-purifying tablets and a couple of his matches dipped in nail polish. They would have been nice to fiddle with anyway.

In our first batch of territory, I started south along a logging road and presently found myself walking northeast. My left foot had begun to hurt. I corrected my course, but presently found myself walking northeast again. This was unaccountable. My left foot was hurting worse.

Brisley and I moved several miles to the Canouse Flowage, a big, wide place in the Canouse River. Again I had a tendency to circle to my left. My left foot hurt more. I began to wish I had Burg's first-aid kit. I could have wondered what to do with it.

Nothing, not even a fresh sign, turned up at the Flowage, and Brisley led me several more miles by car to a batch of thick woods near the St. Croix River. I circled to my left and began to hobble. It would have been nice then to have Burg's transistor radio or his little metal box with flint on the bottom for striking matches. A man can amuse himself with stuff like that when his left foot hurts.

When we got back to Loon Bay Lodge, George Welock, the master of the place, wanted to know what had happened. When he was invited to shut up, he wouldn't do it. He said a woman who is hanging around this lodge had found that her boots were not mates and hadn't been able to get out today at all.

He said her boots were the same color as mine. It turned out that this woman had mixed her boots with mine. No wonder I had been moving to my left all day long. She said the reason she had mixed them was that they were the same color, but the excuse sounded weak, weak.

And to finish everything off, Burg had no folding bootjack to help me get that left boot off. A man ought not to go into the Canadian woods without the proper equipment. Raphael didn't have one either.

To Catch Bass on Mississippi Bayous, Cast Plug at Lizard on a Tree

Pascagoula, Mississippi—The way to catch bass around here is to work along a bayou bank with a sculling machine, find a lizard head-down on a cypress tree, and cast a plug at the lizard.

This is an uncomplicated matter to such a man as Withee Carver of Pascagoula, who was trying out his new sculling machine today. It is called a Hydro-fin, and consists, roughly, of a metal fin manipulated by a rudderlike bar.

It worked so well that Carver, who has been using a paddle on Mississippi bayous all his life, was giving only about nine-tenths of his attention to fishing. The pastime of manipulating a boat with one hand so obsessed him that his attention sometimes wandered from bait-casting for as much as two or three seconds.

Watching it fascinated me, too, and probably that is the reason I had no strikes for three hours. There is no other logical explanation. The fact that Lawton Carver, of New York, Withee Carver's brother, had no strikes in that time either is irrelevant. Lawton Carver, using a fly rod, was trying to catch squirrels: at any rate, he was casting into the cypress trees along the bank frequently.

Withee Carver, too distracted by his new toy to do anything much with fish, had caught nothing but a couple of bass, neither of which weighed more than three pounds, and a fairly good white perch. He regarded this as disgraceful but was too infatuated by his sculling machine to be humiliated.

The lizard awakened him to the hard realities of Mississippi fishing and to the realization that Jackson County expected better things of him. The lizard was flicking about on the bark of a cypress that stood in the water a couple of feet from shore.

Carver instantly forgot the marvels of modern technology.

41

"A bass is going to be lying in the water right under that lizard, waiting for him to lose his holt," he said in tones of ringing authority. And with that he whipped a Garcia Flopy plug at the lizard.

His brother asserts that Carver, using an Ambassador reel, can hit a crawling housefly at twenty yards with a plug. I do not wholly believe this, although Lawton Carver often has been known to tell the truth. But the plug did strike the cypress tree exactly where the lizard had been a fraction of a second before.

The lizard had whipped around the tree, out of sight. The Flopy dropped into the water and immediately vanished in a swirling splash. Carver's six-and-a-half-foot glass casting rod was arched for five minutes or so. A four-pound bass was the result.

I do not like people to call their shots like that. It smacks of virtuosity. And it would be double virtuosity to match or top such stunts. It was essential for me to use restraint for the rest of the day, and I did. So did Lawton Carver. Otherwise, we easily could have caught some fish.

This stunt happened on Portico Bayou (pronounced Potticaw around here). We proceeded then to Johnican Bayou and finally to Ward Bayou—all beautiful, quiet, deep streams flowing between walls of cypress, dogwood, wild pecan, and laurel.

The dogwood was in blossom, and Withee Carver was paying great attention to his favorite tree. He talked so much about it and about his sculling machine that he was able to catch only four or five more bass, none weighing more than three pounds. Lawton Carver wasn't talking much. He seemed to be brooding about something.

What Happened When Dear Old Daddy "Caughten" a Bass Out of Season

It is true that a strong, hardy outdoorsman has a natural obligation to teach his children the lore he thinks he knows and to influence them to respect the game laws, but the trouble is that there are always two or more schools of thought on everything.

For example, when a trout angler has piled all his tackle and gear into a small mountain in the hall of his home and is ready to go fishing, what does he do when his nine-year-old son whines to be taken along?

There are, of course, two schools of thought. One says to take him along and spend the day untangling his tackle. Be a pal, that school says.

The other school says to dismiss him with the serious advice that when a nine-year-old boy wants to go fishing, he ought to go under his own steam. Teach him initiative and self-reliance, says this stern school. It is not true that members of this school simply do not want to be bothered on the stream by the whims of a rattle-headed kid. They simply feel that the school of experience is better than the school of pampering. They are men of strong character.

But who is right? No pattern can be laid down that will suit everybody or even anybody. A boy has his rights, and so has dear old Dad.

Respect for the law is a different matter. The boy must be taught that, and nobody has discharged his duty in that respect more devotedly than a certain respectable citizen of this community who went fishing alone a couple of weeks ago.

He caught a few bullheads, strung them, and hung them in the water to keep fresh, and then caught a black bass. It is illegal to kill black bass in this season of the year, but the respectable citizen found himself unable to return it to the water; he got into some sort of trance and put the fish in his tackle box.

A boat with another fisherman came alongside, and the other fisherman asked about luck. The respectable citizen showed his bullheads. They were duly admired. Then the tackle box began to jump. The respectable citizen muttered something about having his pet rabbit in there, and took off.

When he got home, he showed his string, including the bass, to his family in the privacy of his kitchen.

"Wow!" his six-year-old son remarked, "you caughten a bass!"

Character and solid morals will always come to the front in the moment of stress, sometimes. The respectable citizen recognized a crossroads in his domestic affairs. If he slipped now, his son would never respect the law, and the old man himself would never amount to much around the house again. He did not slip.

"Son," he said kindly but firmly, "it is not 'caughten'; it is 'caught.' You must watch that. And this is not a bass. It is a trout. It is a special kind of pond trout, the name of which escapes me now, but I will look it up in the Museum of Natural History and let you know later.

"Now, son, watch that word 'caughten.' A sportsmanlike fisherman always respects the laws of English as well as game."

The boy was saved for the ranks of sportsmanship and no doubt will grow up to equal or even surpass his father in grammar and outdoor lore. He proved this by his final remark of surprise and pleasure as he turned back to the television set.

"Huh," he said. "It don't look like no trout to me."

Georgia Quail Shooting
That Calls for Some
Lessons in Speed-Sneering

Camilla, Georgia—This was the kind of quail-shooting day that hunters hope to strike once a year, and sometimes strike a good deal more than that in these parts. That means it was a brisk 40 degrees, cloudless, with a light, steady wind to help the dogs.

After a week of hunting in cold, gusty winds, even though there were plenty of birds in the air during those days, it was a treat.

Three hunters picked up twenty-one birds in about three hours of hunting, and might have picked up more than that by hunting singles more thoroughly.

The three pointers in use today found eight coveys, three of which flushed wild ahead of the dogs. Most of them were located either in ground-cover near the edges of woods or just inside open woods. They were all native birds, all fast, tricky fliers. No better shooting could be devised.

Of course, it was something of a trial to be in the company of a couple of experts, in this case C. B. Cox, operator with Woodrow Brooks of the Riverview Shooting Preserve on which we were hunting, and Donald Hays, a neighboring farmer and sometimes a quail guide for the preserve.

These men can't receive any credit for good shooting: they are *supposed* to be able to shoot. It is my fair and reasonable custom to give them two demerits for every shot missed and to charge them a pointer puppy when neither of them totals ten demerits. But they won't pay off.

Yet it is a trial, just the same, for the visiting shooter. Cox and Hays possess an ability shared by almost all shooting-preserve operators and all professional guides. They can sneer

45

without making a sound or moving a face muscle. They use it against all visitors and even against each other.

This gift was brought into play on one occasion when, shooting a double-barreled 12-gauge shotgun, I killed two birds out of three that rose within seconds of each other. Nothing was said, but somehow I got the impression that I should have killed all three or should have been shooting a 20-gauge or even a .410.

At another time I missed a bird in the open twice. I explained carefully to Cox and Hays that a blackberry vine had caught my foot and the sun was almost in my eyes, besides the fact that my right eye hurt and I was shooting low-brass Number 8's when I should have been shooting high-brass Number 9's.

The explanation was accepted, since both Cox and Hays know that a sportsman never offers excuses, only sound reasons; but in some way I had the unreasonable feeling that I should have killed that bird.

This sort of thing is unfair. When Cox or Hays missed a bird, they went on hunting in bitter, sulking silence, refusing to explain why they had missed right there on their own grounds over their own dogs and shooting at birds they had known all their lives. They would even refuse when I kindly cited all these advantages.

But it was a pleasure to watch the dogs, all strong, eager, careful operators, all handling their coveys and singles almost perfectly and backing each other beautifully. They had plenty of work to do: eight coveys in three hours (two or three of them thirty-bird coveys) is as much as any hunter could want when a reasonable number of singles are hunted out in each covey.

The birds and the dogs and the conditions were all ideal. It is too bad the same cannot be said of Cox and Hays. But before I come here again, I am going to take some sneering lessons. I am going to take them from a New York headwaiter and show these Georgia boys what good, sound, copper-riveted, long-distance speed-sneering really is.

Angler Hooked on Figures
Determines Size of
Fishing Haul for 1985

Something has gone wrong with the projected fishing statistics, lovely as they are, and it would be nice if the amateur statisticians would attack the pros, defeat them, and straighten us all out.

The statistics come from different places, but it is said that figures cannot lie, so they must all be true. For example, here comes one from the Senate Select Committee on Water Resources, as quoted by the Associated Fishing Tackle Manufacturers, a trade association that is not necessarily disinterested:

The committee predicted that there would be 47,000,000 persons fishing in the United States by 1980; that they would spend 930,000,000 man-days doing it and pay out $4,500,000,000 for tackle, transportation, lodging, and meals on fishing trips.

Let's see, now. The Democrats hollered in their convention that there were 176,000,000 persons in this country now. And somebody else, I forget who, says there will be 200,000,000 in 1980. That means a gain of 24,000,000. The Tackle Manufacturers say there are 30,000,000 persons fishing this year.

Oh, this is marvelous stuff! Subtracting one thing from another, we find that with a gain of 24,000,000 in population, we are going to gain 17,000,000 fishermen. Why are the Tackle Manufacturers going to allow 7,000,000 free-born Americans not to fish?

Then again, the 24,000,000 population gain is 14 per cent. But the 17,000,000 gain in fishermen will be 70 per cent of the population gain. Is the Senate going to enforce this?

I can't do anything about those 930,000,000 man-days, which are the number of days it would take one man to fish 2,547,945 years, if there were no leap years and I didn't get lost in arithmetic. But a good amateur statistician ought to be able to spend a week with them and come up with something pretty ripe.

But back to business. Some statisticians say that 30,000,000 fishermen spend $3,000,000,000 on fishing now, $250,000,000 of it on tackle alone. If 47,000,000 fishermen, or 56.6 per cent more, are going to spend only $4,500,000,000, or only 50 per cent more, does this mean deflation? Has the Senate got other and bigger plans for the economy, outside fishing? There are grave implications here.

The simple, or nonstatistical mind keeps roaming back to those 930,000,000 man-days and trying feebly to get some sort of hold on them. How long would it have taken Caesar's legions to use them up? If Rome was not built in a day, how many man-days was Rome built in?

If it took a writer 500 days to write a good book, 1,920,000 classics could be written in those man-days. But if a man can catch 2 pounds of fish in a man-day, 1,920,000,000 pounds of fish will be taken by sportsmen in 1980, which is more to the point at issue.

Now we are getting to something solid. Between 1980 and 1985, at that rate, even if the fishing population suddenly stops growing, 9,600,000,000 pounds of sports fish will be caught, or 4,800,000 tons. This is good news.

Outdoorsmen Test Strong
Constitutions Indoors
on Stories of Derring-Do

Colrain, Massachusetts—This is the stagnant backwater of the year when a strong, hardy outdoorsman can't find anything to be strong or hardy about and must therefore read he-man magazines.

This literature will maintain in him the spirit of the wild as he sits beside a window and watches the loose snow blowing outside. It is full of crafty outdoor stratagems and narrow escapes from death.

And after reading the story entitled "How I Outwitted the Ol' Lunker," he can figure out unerringly what really did happen. The story outline runs like this:

Strong Hardy Outdoorsman locates gigantic brown trout in eddy under high cutbank across roaring stream ten feet above twenty-foot falls. Ol' Lunker is famous; everybody in state has tried for him.

S. H. Outdoorsman studies O. L. for three weeks through glasses, discovers he is rising to fly unknown to entomology or to fly-tiers. S. H. O. whips out field-tying kit, cunningly ties exact imitation. Wades into stream, which is soon up to armpits and very powerful. But invincible love of fishing and adventure keep him going.

Finally gets within reach of ninety-foot cast and drops perfect fly in perfect position ahead of O. L. Water erupts and strike almost tears S. H. O.'s arm from shoulder. Wild emotion. He starts playing fish perfectly, but foot catches in rock-crack and line whips around his neck as he goes down in fast water only eight feet above falls.

Love of fishing and adventure make him hang on, and he is about to drown obstinately when he remembers he used to be contortionist. Uses old circus trick to free foot and stand up-right at edge of falls. Fish has gone over falls. S. H. O. re-members he used to do levitation magic on Keith circuit, skill-fully plays fish up over falls (or goes down to him hanging on willow branches). Lands him. Fourteen pounds, three ounces.

Housebound Strong Hardy Outdoorsman, reading this, knows immediately what happened:

Author fished three hours with random flies, got no strike. Switched to spinning tackle with fifteen-pound test line and hard-ware lures. Nothing happened for two more hours.

Author tired and disgusted. Sits on rock in flat stretch of stream, lights cigarette, tosses bait morosely in general direction of opposite bank. Monofilament twists around reel base. Author curses, gets into coughing spell while trying to smoke and uses both hands freeing monofilament.

Trout picks up hardware from bottom and swallows it, un-noticed by author. Rod tip begins to jerk and he finally notices it, but monofilament is not freed from reel. He discards rod and pulls in fish hand-over-hand. Two-pound, three-ounce brown.

Any angler can boil that written story down to its basis. And any angler knows what the last sentence of the story will say:

"If you want the Ol' Lunkers, you have to work for them."

Survey Fails to Disclose
Any Sensible Reasons
for Enjoying Fishing

A basic question has been bothering everybody around here lately, mainly because all the answers given are false and in-sincere. The question is: Why do people go fishing?

It is too bad the answer is not so obvious as the answer to: Why do men become explorers? Explorers are timid men. They want to know how they look in beards but do not have the crust to grow them at home. So they go to the headwaters of the Orinoco and grow beards. This is self-evident.

But nobody can give a believable, or even honest, answer about fishing, though everybody seems to have some kind of answer.

For example, some say they fish to get fish. Obviously false. There are enough fish-hogs around for any reasonable purpose, of course. But how about these fellows who never take a fish?

There is a story about one Boston angler who won't even use hooks. For a while he tried barbless hooks and would bring a fish to netting distance, then give him slack and let him wriggle off. For a while his esthetic principles were satisfied, but even this became too crude.

Now he will use only dry flies without hooks. He wants only the strike, and if the fish strikes anywhere except in the place the angler has chosen, he is dissatisfied. This man lives in Maine and, to make things tougher, will now fish only for bonefish, because Florida is far away and bonefish are warier than trout.

Obviously his next step is to eliminate the lure and in the end he is bound to refine himself out of existence, if any. But he certainly is not fishing to get fish.

And there is the character on Long Island who, after days of futile trying for stripers, got strike after strike on a hookless plug. When he wanted the bass, he said, the bass didn't want him; now the bass wanted him and to hell with them. Does this guy want fish?

What about the angler who says he just loves the outdoors and refers to nature as "She"? That can't be his reason for fishing. Anybody can mess around in the woods and observe stuff without annoying fish.

And the one who says it is a reflective sport? Twaddle. The place for that contemplation kick is a leather-upholstered easy chair, with pipe, smoking jacket, stone fireplace, and beautiful setter looking up with adoring eyes at The Master. Who can muckle onto any philosophical speculation while breaking his ankle on rough rocks, blistering his hands on oars, or scratching black-fly bites?

What about the one who goes for good fellowship? Can't be that. He can get that in church organizations, fraternal orders, clubs, and chess tournaments. If that is not his pitch, New York City itself has superb, even unexampled facilities for playing poker, shooting dice, and drinking whisky. A man doesn't have to go to the hot, fly-blown woods to get drunk or go broke.

Is fishing good exercise? Tennis or swimming is better. Does it get a person out in the fresh air? So does opening a door.

There are those who say the lure lies in catching the biggest and the most, beating everybody else. With enough practice they can do the same on pinball machines.

Some say they want to pit their skill and cunning against Nature. Like the man who says he has "conquered" a mountain when he has crawled up the side of it. So do ants conquer drainpipes.

Anyway, that can't really be his reason for going fishing. Nature makes things easy with soft days and willing fish, and he makes them easier with expensive and ingenious tackle. Anyway, he could go climb a mountain: fish are not Nature; they're just natural, except when they are hatchery pets.

This survey uncovered, or exposed, anglers who say the great attraction is manipulating tackle and even mending rods and tying flies. Well, very fine tackle manipulators can be seen in any casting contest, but they are not catching fish. Many of them never go fishing, but the confusing thing is that many of them do.

And many thousands of Americans, including housewives, tie flies, but do not fish. Many of them do fish, but it can't be because they tie flies, since that would make the fishing only an almost irrelevant by-product.

Well, the survey didn't get anywhere. Sometimes it seemed as if the right answer was about to appear, but it didn't. Nobody was thinking in a detached, scientific manner; everybody just seemed to want to justify his fishing—as if his wife were listening.

But I am going to think about it tomorrow in a detached, scientific manner. While fishing.

Old Myth Exploded:
Country Boys Fail to Beat
Adult in Trout Fishing

Bernardston, Massachusetts—At long last, as kings say when they blow their jobs, a vicious old canard has been exposed, exploded, and expunged. Country boys equipped with aboriginal tackle do not always catch the most and biggest fish, and sometimes they catch no fish at all.

The miserable old myth, a libel on both the innocence of youth and the outdoor sophistication of modern American manhood, was nailed irrevocably today on the banks of the little Falls River here. It can never again be given credence by anybody except calendar and magazine-cover artists.

Like many events of transcending importance, this one almost passed unnoticed, though for many generations grown men have been snarling in fury at the notion that children outfish them.

For two hours I had been fishing the Falls River, a little stream that flows pleasantly through meadows here. It is ordinarily quiet, proceeding gently along over gravel bars and through small and shallow holes in a course lined with willows almost all the way. But rains early this week had swelled it. Now it races high, swift, and noisy.

There were no fly hatches today that I could see. It was difficult to handle a wet fly, and as far as I was concerned there was no profit in it. A red-and-yellow streamer had brought to hook one six-inch brook trout. But he must have been a subnormal, underprivileged, delinquent fish; at any rate, he did not conform, he had no notion of togetherness or belongingness. None of his little playmates was striking, or even rising.

This situation called for worms, and I would have used worms if I had had any. The ground was wet, too, and worms must have been near the top. But I didn't happen to see a shovel

53

lying around anywhere, and a couple of kids I asked to dig for me weren't interested in two bits. They were sweating out their driving licenses.

So I kept on hurling streamers, sometimes changing hopelessly to a wet fly and sometimes just wading morosely along the Falls River. It appeared to be a black day, and little would any man have guessed that the moment of revelation was at hand, that a truth of Nature was about to be discovered, or bared.

Two boys came ambling along downstream, as aimless and abstracted as any other twelve-year-old boys on any trout stream. Mark this: one of them had a new spinning outfit and was casting hardware; the other was equipped casually with an ancient steel fly rod, cuttyhunk line, and worms.

They were a double threat, the modern and the old-time boy, but that kid with the worms was more than a threat: he was imminent disaster. By the book, he was bound to have a limit of big fish.

Neither of those delinquents had a single trout. They had been fishing for hours and hadn't registered a bite. I questioned them closely and in depth, and they had every advantage that a calendar artist could dream up at his corniest.

Both were local country boys, reared (so far) on farms. Both were absent from school without any kind of permission. Both knew every stone in the river, and had been trying to catch a trout out of it since the age of five. Both wore country clothes, though neither wore overalls, since to do so would have revealed their intentions to their parents when they left home ostensibly for school.

There was one minor fault: neither was barefooted. But the day was chilly, and again, a boy can't leave home in the morning barefooted when his purpose is to skip school.

They didn't even have any evident hope of catching a trout. I had caught a trout, and I don't want to hear any more about these country boys with bent pins. A boy is a pleasing thing, without his switchblade, but he is not a man.

Success With Makeshift Fishing Tackle Puts Another Soul on Road to Ruin

If there is any one thing that a strong, hardy outdoorsman likes more than another, it is to catch a fish on some unusual makeshift tackle. Let a man use a ping-pong ball for a float and catch a fish that way and he becomes insufferable.

There used to be a boy in my neighborhood who bored a hole on a tablespoon, snapped off the handle, tied on a hook, and caught a pickerel with it. It was the ruination of that boy. He already was a fairly mouthy kid, but after that he couldn't stop talking. He got to hanging around pool halls and wound up a lecturer. But it didn't matter much to his folks by then; they already had disowned him.

So there was George Dourdounas preening himself as he mixed milk shakes and stuff at Mike Manuche's on Second Avenue. On the bar in front of him lay a three-pound, smallmouth black bass with a popping bug still in its mouth and an odd-looking leader tied to the popping bug.

There were people present who said the bass had been there every night for nearly two weeks, but that is not so. Dourdounas' days off had been only five days before. And Manuche had passed a rule that Dourdounas could show the bass only for two hours each evening.

The trick behind this bass was that it had been caught on a dental-floss leader, with a fly rod. Dourdounas had taken the fish at his place on Lake Nuangola, near Wilkes-Barre, Pennsylvania, in the presence of an admiring audience made up of his wife and three children.

He was telling all hands that dental floss makes the finest bass leader known to mankind. He said it tested at twenty pounds and was just the stuff for handling a big bass in lily pads and weeds. He said the wax on it made it float pretty good for a while, but that after an hour or so it started to sink. He said that was just what was needed. He said his three-pounder had tried to snarl him in the lily pads, but that the strong floss had allowed him to horse the fish through them.

He said he never was going to fish for bass again with anything except dental floss. He said he was going to try it on trout, too. He said there was no limit to the possibilities of the thing.

Under his compelling eye, everybody admired the bass, except maybe Mike Manuche, and Dourdounas was able to elicit nineteen testimonials to the dental floss, including one from a cadaverous blond clothes model who first had to be told what a leader was. She had it confused at first with President Eisenhower.

By one of these million-to-one chances that can happen only in a great metropolis, one of the men drinking milk shakes there happened to be the press agent for Johnson & Johnson, a medical-supply house that just happens to make the dental floss Dourdounas had used to catch the bass. He had been standing there for five days.

Hunters Fail to Bag Bobcat
or Deer, but Get to Know
Numerous Auto Mechanics

The marvels of modern technology are in truth a great aid to the modern hunter, but sometimes it seems as if a man might do better to stay at home in an old-fashioned rocker reading a good old-fashioned comic book. Look at the record of a very recent deer and bobcat hunting trip to New Hampshire.

A party of four started in a two-year-old car owned by one of them. He had traded it in, but the modern technologists of Detroit were three weeks late in delivering the new car. After

56

about a hundred and fifty miles, the one in use developed a steering-wheel shudder.

A modern technologist in a Massachusetts garage diagnosed the trouble with instant authority as something to do with bushings in the steering box. It sounded like he said bushings, anyway; might have said camshaft or eccentric or worm gear or something technological like that.

In any case, he fixed it and it shuddered worse. Another modern technologist in a New Hampshire garage stated with instant authority that the first modern technologist was a bum and that the trouble was in the wheels. Nobody caught the specific detail of this, but it was pretty technological. The car was fixed again.

The party had been scheduled to start deer hunting at 10 A.M. and it was now 2 P.M. There was fine deer hunting all around, and it would have been nice to start then, but the car began to shudder so violently that it could be driven no more than ten miles an hour.

Somehow the car was nursed to a bigger town, which cherished a dealer in that make of car. This modern technologist stated with instant authority that the trouble was in the differential and that it would take about four days to fix it. The car was left there, and its owner called his home in White Plains to explain his predicament to his family. He was cordially informed that his new car was ready.

A second member of the party had a car in the New Hampshire area where the party had intended to hunt. It had been left there with a friend. The party went to get it, although the deer-hunting project was by now dead.

It had a flat tire, and the trunk containing the spare was locked. Its owner took the tire off and toted it to a local garage, which was closed. The garage operator was phoned and showed up to fix the tire. He also provided four quarts of antifreeze.

The tire was replaced and the car started. A half hour later its owner lighted a match to see whether the radiator was still full, and the antifreeze caught fire. The fire was extinguished with snow. A little later both antifreeze and water boiled out.

It was then 1 A.M. and bobcat hunting was slated for 7 A.M. The hunters got something to eat, drained the radiator and block, and went to bed at 2 A.M. At 6 A.M. a modern technologist who had been called in advance by telephone opened his filling station and with instant authority diagnosed the trouble: the freeze-plug had rusted through. He did not have another. The car was left there for the day, and the hunters proceeded in a rented car and vainly hunted bobcats. The car was ready that evening, and held water.

Nobody got shot. Nobody broke a leg. One member of the party changed a diaper for a young mother who had to leave her baby for a few minutes. That was a marvel of old-time technology.

It's Easy to Climb Down
a Forty-Foot Bank, but Don't
Trust Rocks in Fast Water

Andover, New Hampshire—Nothing makes an outdoor type feel so strong and so hardy as the knowledge that he has endured stoically a rude knock and thereby earned the applause of his companions. A visible bruise or cut, casually dismissed as a mere trifle, is a badge of honor.

A man can earn his badges on the Blackwater River if he exercises due carelessness. In some places, there are fine slippery rocks in fast water and good steep banks covered with brush and vines that offer unexcelled opportunities for minor injuries.

One of these is just below a certain bridge, in a fast riffle running between a falls and a deep pool. The bank leading to this riffle is about forty feet high and covered with loose dirt. The rocks below are irregular and slippery enough for all practical purposes.

The motives of John Brennan of the New Hampshire Planning and Industrial Commission in sending fishermen down this bank are not known. He is not a brutal type, and the publicity the state might win by the maiming of a single angler probably wouldn't be worth the trouble, unless fishing were particularly dull. Brennan says he sends them down because there are good brookies in that riffle, and there are, and maybe that is his reason.

Anyway, I was able to negotiate that bank with the agility, sure foot, and stout heart of a mountain goat. At the moment I wasn't even looking for honorable bruises, since there was nobody around to impress except Brennan. And he has been known to ignore a man with a broken leg in order to watch another catch an eight-inch trout.

The rocks at the bottom were equally easy to negotiate for an experienced rock-jumper. But somebody had moved one of them, and, when I stepped down onto it, there was nothing there except a patch of black water. If anybody could have recovered his balance at that instant, I probably could have; but nobody could.

The resulting flat dive onto the remaining rocks was executed with skill and grace. Some men might have been hurt, but not an old rock-faller. I even managed skillfully to lodge my six-and-a-half-foot Orvis bamboo rod in a willow bush on the way down, and to secure it there firmly by twining the leader among the branches.

That strategy freed my hands and enabled me to hit those rocks so softly that I was able to get up in less than ten minutes. It took me less than another ten minutes to free the rod.

Brennan watched this performance with admiration. He said that to fall in a place like that, I must have practiced rock-falling a lot. He said he had been down that bank thirty-eight times and had never been able to fall at all. He said he was fairly sure that he had seen people who were noisier after a fall like that, though he couldn't recall at the moment who they were. Brennan doesn't mind saying he likes a thing when he does.

Well, I caught eight good brookies, a couple of them weighing about a pound, in that riffle with a leader carrying two wet flies, rigged by Harry Darbee of Roscoe, New York. They were all natives and all full of fight.

That took me about an hour. Probably it was standing in one position all that time that made me begin to shake a little after the hour. But it was no great job getting up the bank again, and Brennan really didn't have to help.

He didn't have to say anything about how a man ought to know his own limits, either. There are certain badges of honor that could be shown to him, if I didn't scorn to do it.

To Shoot Buck Behind
Left Shoulder, Aim There
and Stumble

Township 24, Washington County, Maine—These Maine deer are about as unaccountable as the tough and intrepid outdoorsmen who pursue them, and that at times is very unaccountable.

On our first drive today through a swamp lying between blueberry barrens, we saw two hunters sitting on a large boulder on a slope far away fire a dozen times at a buck at least a quarter of a mile from them. The buck did not seem disturbed; just ambled away into some maple sprouts.

In the next couple of hours we drove through two or three of those swamps, all of them places that have produced deer in the past. There were no deer in any of them, or in the thickets of sprouts through which we frequently passed.

Six of us were returning to the truck that had brought us as near as possible to the swamps we had just investigated. Stillman Look, the big, sharp-eyed guide who runs Dan Hartford's Camp with George Drisko, was in the lead a step or two ahead of me.

We were no more than a hundred yards from the truck, in open blueberry barren, when a buck burst from a little rick hole no bigger than a medium-sized Second Avenue bar. A rick hole, in the parlance of this region, is a shallow cup of damp land containing a few sprouts and maybe a dead birch or so.

Look was carrying no rifle. I had a Winchester Model 88, lever action, .243 caliber, with a four-power Weaver telescope on a slide mount. It is possible to dismount the scope quickly in thick brush and mount it again quickly in the open. At the moment, it was mounted.

The buck jumped out across the barrens, running across our path. When the rifle came up, he seemed to jump into the scope. I aimed behind his left shoulder, but I must have stepped into a hole or something, because the bullet caught him behind the left shoulder. He piled up there, dragged himself a few yards, and was dispatched with the next shot.

Hunters and guides gathered around the buck, an eleven-pointer that later weighed two hundred and eight pounds field-dressed. Bud Leavitt, sports editor and columnist of the Bangor *Daily News,* carefully unloaded his rifle. He doesn't like loaded rifles when people are standing around.

A few minutes later Leavitt was returning to the truck when a large doe jumped from the same little rick hole. She had stayed there quietly in all the doings of the last half hour. Leavitt was caught without a clip in his rifle.

But four strangers who had come up to the truck and were standing there were not caught that way. All four started firing at the doe, and they fired past Leavitt, their bullets coming within a dozen feet of him. Leavitt ducked and forgot about getting a clip into his rifle. None of the four touched the doe.

Leavitt killed a doe a little later in the day but didn't feel much like hunting anyway. He seemed abstracted during the afternoon. Not even Mrs. Gladys Mace, the amiable storekeeper at Aurora who tags five hundred deer a year, could tease him into teasing her. This is a record that will stand for years.

Hunters Stalk the Killing
Remark, Then Load the
Conversation to Drop It

Now that the hunting season is at hand, the day of the deathless sentence, adorned by the artfully emphasized word, is also about to dawn. Hunters, by any fair count, are better at this art, although a rare fisherman can be pretty good at times.

Take the old Vermont angler observed on the Battenkill near Shushan, New York, by Okey Butcher of Shushan, purveyor of trapping supplies. Butcher watched him, unseen from the bank only a few feet away.*

The old man, presenting a tiny dry fly with delicate skill, rose a very small trout three times and tried again with unhurried patience. This time he hooked the little thing and, standing alone in the river, or so he thought, addressed the midget.

"Wall, I guess, by Godfrey, I straighten YOU out," he said.

A poker-playing turkey hunter at Claiborne, Alabama, last spring uttered a sentence with more solid construction in it. He had called up a gobbler on his cedar-and-slate turkey-call, and missed it at twenty-five yards with a shotgun.

The bird ran away with the speed of light, never taking to wing. The hunter must have been building a good sentence all the way back to the hunting lodge. First he admitted that he hadn't got a turkey. Then he added:

"I called one up and bet into him, hoping he'd drop," the man said, "but he called ME and won with a pair of legs."

That one was all rounded out and and showed clearly that some thought had been put into it by a man who took pride in his work.

An old man who worked on the farm of Winfield Scott Lyons, Jr., at Edgewater Beach, Maryland, a few years ago showed

62

what age and experience could do with only a few minutes' preparation.

He was watching a couple of young beagles in training pursue a rabbit. The rabbit ran up a little knoll covered with low dewberry vines, in sight of three of us, made a couple of doubles, jumped sideways six feet, and snaked into a woodpile.

The young dogs came up and couldn't untangle the line. The old man watched them casting about uncertainly for a few minutes while he worked up his sentence.

"That rabbit," he said with the deceptively casual air of the practiced thinker of witticisms, "has done come up here and played a card THEM dogs can't trump."

Sometimes a younger man, by quick thinking, can pull himself out of the hole with a good sentence. Last winter, while hunting from River Forest Manor at Belhaven, North Carolina, Axson Smith, operator of the lodge, and I watched a goose come in and land among the decoys, get up, and fly away again. Each of us expected the other to shoot, and the goose got away. I asked Smith, a little indignantly, why he hadn't shot. His answer:

"I was waiting for you to MISS him first.

Some Rules of Behavior for Outdoorsmen Who Happen to Be Snowed In

Colrain, Massachusetts—Iron convention and the painted midwinter covers of all magazines dictate that, when there is two feet of snow on the ground, the American outdoorsman must get out his fly-fishing tackle and work over it in the comfort of his habitation. Stories inside the magazine say he does it lovingly, so he must contrive a way to get some enjoyment out of this curious and tedious duty.

63

There are two feet of snow on the ground now, and there can be no harm in giving this man some guidance from time to time on how to follow the imperious commands of magazine covers. At least he can do it in such a way as to insure domestic tranquility.

First, he should choose a room that is well lighted and, above all, used constantly by other members of the family, such as high-school daughters with dates. A man gets lonesome in a den or trophy room, and there is no point in going through this ceremony without witnesses. Alone, whom would the outdoorsman impress?

Clear a table of books, ash trays, old letters, bills, calendars, pictures, tablets, stationeries, handbags, vases, and knickknacks, and substitute any other lamp for the lamp already on it. Spread on its surface containers of oil of various thicknesses, tubes of graphite and glue, oily rags, sandpaper, pliers, and any other small tools in the house.

Wives rarely complain about this, though some look a little grim. If the wife does complain, a thousand magazine stories have dictated that the outdoorsman puff his pipe clumsily and smile tolerantly, for she is only a cute little saucepot showing her femininity.

Get out the fly rods and assemble them at table. There is nothing wrong with them, but study them critically. Poke a little wedge of sandpaper into a few line-guides. This looks quite expert and can do no harm.

Stop now and demand coffee, especially if nobody is paying attention. This is necessary stage business, but do not carry it too far. Put the pipe away. It has served its purpose, and there is no sense getting sicker.

At this point it is a good idea for the outdoorsman to offer to take his wife on a fishing trip next summer. This will please her because it is some kind of an offer. If she likes to fish, she means to go anyway; if not, she can think about rooting around in rebuilt barns for worthless discards she calls antiques.

Put the rods back in their cases and get out two reels. Study them critically and test line tension by pulling on the line. If the outdoorsman feels especially energetic, he can put a drop or two of oil in various oil holes. Then he can resolve to take the reels to a tackle shop for cleaning and overhaul. He may even do it the day before the fishing season opens, when the tackle shops are full of reels for overhaul.

That is about all. Put the rods and reels away, but do not pick up the oils and tools and other stuff. Leave it there. Keep it firmly in mind that women dislike and distrust neat men; they regard a certain amount of disorder as manly. Besides, the high-school girl's date may be impressed, or want to use some of the gun oil on his hair. The outdoorsman has done his magazine-cover duty; the debris is beneath his notice.

Larcenous Fly-Tiers Fail in Efforts to Find Out Secrets of the Art

Fly-tying trout fishermen are now turning their homes into nightime sweatshops for the production of wet and dry flies to be used as soon as the season opens. There are several sound methods for nontying fishermen to get flies away from these people. None of them works.

It is not that fly-tiers are stingy with their work, which they are. It is simply that in them burns the fiercest creative pride on earth. They cannot bring themselves to surrender their masterpieces.

It ought not to be that way. Art needs appreciation; a tier ought to give flies to his nontying friends, and let them be seen by the world. Did Leonardo hide his works? But they won't do it. They show the flies, brag about them, make nontiers feel ill-equipped, and hoard them.

There is a fellow in Ossining, for example, who has a fly-tying machine. It is only an ordinary fly vise, but it is equipped with pencil-sharpener handles, parts of electric-light sockets, universal joints, and other things. He can put a rooster feather in one end, grind the pencil-sharpener handle, and take a light Cahill out of the other end. He wouldn't give his grandmother one of them. The best way to work on a tier is to flatter him and at the same time poor-mouth him. That doesn't work either, but it comes closest. This is about the way it goes:

Tier just happens to have in pocket cardboard box loaded with beautiful flies he has tied. Hauls the flies out one at a time, counting them every fifteen seconds, and says:

"Look at that hackle! Got it from a guy in Nevada that grows his own chickens and won't let anybody have hackle but me. These are terrific! Tied 'em last night. Look how they stand up! You can't buy flies like these!"

Nontier tries: "Gee, terrific! Look at that hackle. Where'd you get it? Best I ever seen! I can't buy flies like that! Look how they stand up! Gee! I can't get flies like that; wish I could. Wish I could tie like that. Hands are too clumsy, and I ain't got the patience or the taste. Don't know enough about flies, either, like you do.

"Gee! How long'd it take you to learn that? Wish I could do it. Terrific! Trouble is, I can't buy no good flies. And since I can't tie flies either, I just have to fish with third-rate stuff. Sure would like to fish just once with good flies."

He might even go a little further, and ask if he couldn't buy a few of these creations, or trade for them. But it won't do him any good. The tier will just say he couldn't think of selling. That would be commercial and he just tied these things for pleasure.

Then he will keep those flies out on the table and go on about them, and how he tied them, and where he got the materials, and how no matter which way you drop them they always come up on their noses, and how many of them he has at home, until nobody can stay in the same room with him.

Nobody but the nontier, that is. This poor fellow will keep on desperately poor-mouthing.

This is sorry business. It makes a man lose faith in human nature, unless he is a fly-tier. Fly-tiers who are properly fawned on ought to say:

"You like these? Lemme send you a couple dozen. What the heck [snapping fingers], they're only flies. I can make all I want."

Well, a nontier can dream, can't he?

Sportsman's Reward Has
Its Own Virtue: Donor
Will Name and Keep Trophy

One more award won't hurt the world irretrievably, or make the award industry any sillier than it is. But this is going to be a sensible award; that is, it will be named for the recipient, or awardee, and the donor will keep the trophy.

The special virtue of this arrangement is that the donor can donate a one-hundred-thousand-dollar cabin cruiser and still have it. And if no donor can be found with that much scratch, the awardee can give something to himself to fit the purse, keep it, and still have the honor.

It is a pleasure therefore to announce the Outstanding Fred Brisley Award for the Outstanding Outdoor Sportsman's Remark of 1957. Brisley has performed an outstanding service to outdoor sports and sportsmen by his outstanding remark, which will always serve as an infallible guide to canoe fishermen when a man is overboard.

Brisley is a professional fishing and hunting guide, working for George Welock at his Loon Bay Lodge on the St. Croix River in New Brunswick. He is a man of many remarks, some of them outstanding.

He made his Outstanding Remark of the Year while poling a dude down Haycock Rip, a rapids just above Welock's place. Brisley had shut off the three-horsepower Evinrude and was working the canoe downstream when an outstanding piece of pulpwood struck it and swung the stern end outward.

Haycock Rip is no piece of water to sail sideways, and Brisley couldn't swing the canoe back with the pole. So he went overboard, seized the stern, braced against a rock, and was maneuvering the craft shoreward when the dude in the bow looked around and found himself alone.

"Hey, Brisley, where are you?" he inquired in anxious tones.

This itself would certainly have been the Outstanding Remark of the Year, but Brisley saw his danger of losing the honor and promptly topped it.

"Well, I don't just know," the Outstanding Brisley replied reasonably, spitting out a mouthful of the St. Croix, "but if you know where the propeller of this motor is, you'll have me pretty well located. It's down the front of my pants."

And with that he moved the canoe to the rocks in shallow water, disengaged himself from the propeller, climbed aboard, and took the dude on down through Haycock Rip. He did it with the air of a master of ceremonies who tolerates no heckling from the peasants out there eating chicken à la king at an outstanding dinner.

I am going to present the Outstanding Award to Brisley next time I see him if he has found somebody to donate it or has bought it himself. It is to be expected that such a gifted man will make a graceful, outstanding acceptance speech, full of favorable mention of the outstanding glories of the Great Outdoors. He'll do it, too.

This is a great thing, a fine, warm thing. Everybody can have an outstanding award now. Let man honor man in outstanding brotherhood.

In the South, Midwest, and New England, Every Worm Has His Day

Colrain, Massachusetts—Clinical tests conducted here today proved that angleworms of the South and Midwest are intellectually and emotionally more sensitive than those of New England but do not necessarily catch more fish. One researcher made the bold corollary conclusion that New England fish are less sensitive than Southern and Midwestern fish but might catch more worms.

The research team, which made its findings almost accidentally while pursuing a different study, was composed of Mrs. Liza Fosburgh, formerly of Moultrie, Georgia, but now of Cherry Plain, New York, and Bob Panuska of Cincinnati, a freshman at Williams College. There were several official observers.

The project was begun when Mrs. Fosburgh stated a Georgia scientific axiom that earthworms would erupt hastily from the earth when a driven stake was caused to vibrate by rubbing the top of it with the side of an axe blade.

She stated that Moultrie worms would do it every time. Panuska subscribed to the scientific principle and swore by the grizzled head of William Tecumseh Sherman that Cincinnati worms would do it, too.

Clayt Seagears of Cherry Plain, director of conservation education for New York State, took the position that the Fosburgh-Panuska theory was medievalism, long since disproved by the revelations of quantum mathematics. He argued brilliantly that he would be dad-burned if that stuff was true.

Peter Fosburgh, husband to Liza, kept a diplomatic tongue in his head, loyally ready to rally to his wife's side if worms appeared but leaving a clear line of retreat. One of Panuska's classmates at Williams, naturally, took the intellectual position that the theory could not be sound if Panuska thought it was. Mrs. Marian Seagears adopted the stance of an impartial umpire.

A stake was driven in soft ground where worms had been dug the day before by the Williams scholars. Mrs. Fosburgh crouched beside it and rubbed the axe head briskly across the top of it for fifteen minutes. The ground vibrated. No worms appeared. She said the ground wasn't soft enough.

The process was repeated in fourteen different spots, with Panuska expertly relieving Mrs. Fosburgh at the rubbing. No worms appeared for the following reasons, supplied by Mrs. Fosburgh and Panuska:

The stakes weren't the right size. The axe was not sharp. It had tape on its handle. There was too much grass around. There were no worms in this region anyway. The ground had been grazed over by sheep, and worms didn't like sheep. New England worms were stupid, insensitive creatures not to be compared with the worms of Moultrie and Cincinnati.

The Williams louts filled two cans with worms from the same spot, went off to the nearby Green River, caught four pretty fair brook trout apiece in two hours.

Mrs. Fosburgh concluded logically that the fish hereabouts are as rockheaded as the worms, will bite anything, and therefore probably catch more worms.

Panuska said Cincinnati worms are well known to be of a superior type. Seagears said Einstein had been proved right. Panuska's classmate sneered for a solid hour. Fosburgh withdrew to prepared positions.

Mrs. Seagears ruled impartially that the worms of Colrain, Massachusetts, would not respond to axehead rubbing.

Wherein Invincible
Justice Catches Up With
Overconscientious Warden

Fish River Lake, Maine—This truthful hunting story concerns misfortune, ill judgment, persecution, and the final triumph of justice the invincible.

It was told by John Maines of the Great Northern Paper Company and confirmed by Morris R. Wing of the International Paper Company, both Maine men and both respected as hunters who will always, or often, tell the naked truth about hunting without coercion, or with very little.

The protagonist of the story was a young warden who had the misfortune to discover a grandmother of eighty-five winters sitting high in an apple tree at midnight, a rifle in one hand and a flashlight in the other. He might have escaped his fate by running away, but he was fool enough to do his duty.

A few days later he brought the revered lady into court and charged her with attempting to take deer with the aid of a jacklight. The light, the rifle, and the time o'clock, he said, were prima-facie evidence of her guilt—the chump.

Taking the stand in her own defense and as her own attorney, the ancient lady said she didn't know it was agin the law to set in a tree and gather apples for her husband's Sunday apple pie. She said she did it at night because sun hurt her pore ol' eyes.

Why did she pick apples after frost, when they were all withered? Because she made the best pies out of that kind of apples, she said, and she would like to see the woman, especially these here modern immature do-nothings, who could make as good an apple pie.

Why did she have the light? Well, she would like to see anybody in that courtroom climb an apple tree without a light when they were eighty-five years old.

Why the rifle? Why, to protect herself from bears. And besides, her husband liked a bear steak for dinner now and then, and there wasn't no closed season on bears, and the pore ol' man couldn't get around good enough to climb trees and shoot bears now, so she had to do it, and no immature modern do-nothing could do that kind of thing.

Well, the judge thought it over and convicted her, and fined her fifty dollars, sentence suspended. He knew well enough why she was up that tree, and he would have fined her more except that it was November and the fine was off. In Maine, the fine is off when the season is on and the fine is on when the season is over.

But the warden was lost beyond redemption. How can a man operate in public after arresting an eighty-five-year-old grandmother out of an apple tree and hauling her into court?

A month or two later when he was on a party searching for a lost dude in the woods, somebody asked in his presence if they were likely to meet any babies. A knowing companion fed this man the cue: Well, probably not, but why?

Well, he said, if they met a baby, it might get sent to the penitentiary. They had a man present—didn't they?—who would drag a pore ol' grandmaw out of an apple tree where she was picking fruit for her crippled ol' husband's dinner, and hale her into court and get her fined, make a criminal outen her.

A helpless baby would be an even easier prey for that kind of a man, he said. He, the speaker, wouldn't like his baby daughter to meet up with such a man in the woods. Why, the pore little brat might get ten years.

Nobody around here knows what has happened to that warden.

That was invincible justice. They say it will come every time to a man who administers the law without mercy.

Multiple-Nymph Fishing
Counsel Drives Adviser
Into Troubled Waters

Something about this story of a confirmed joker is worrisome, because it is impossible to determine just who fooled whom and whether he was trying to do it. But it may revolutionize nymph fishing, though the chances are against it.

Anyway, a fly fisherman who works in a midtown office got a call from an acquaintance who had got the notion that he was something of a fishing wizard and who frequently sought his advice. The fly man had sent his caller to various good trout streams in New York and New England and often gave him guidance on lures.

This time the man wanted to get some inside stuff on how to fish a nymph. His adviser had seldom fished a nymph (he was a dry-fly man and tier), but was constitutionally unable to admit it. He was also constitutionally unable to be serious for more than a minute at a time.

Whatever his motives, he advised his friend that he had had great success by tying four nymphs of different patterns to his leader in a bunch. He said it was a killer. He said it never failed. He didn't say he had never tried it.

Conscience smote him a few hours later, but he couldn't locate his friend by phone to straighten him out. He fretted about it for a weekend, confessed to his wife, who duly condemned him as heartless and unfunny, and he worried about what he could do in penance.

Then came a letter from his pupil, and at length he summoned enough character to open it. It said:

> After thinking over how well you did by tying four nymphs in a bunch at the end of your leader, it occurred to me that I might hope to do even better by tying ten to the end of mine. This I did. Eight were bunched very closely together, but two draggled out at the sides of the conglomeration.
>
> I managed to heave-cast the cluster into one of my favorite big pools. When the lures were taken down deep by the current, a big fish struck hard. Luckily, I was fishing a heavy leader. Condensing the struggle, I'll just say that I landed a five-pound rainbow that had taken the middle eight nymphs in one gulp.
>
> On the other two I found a native and a brown, each exactly thirteen and one-half inches long. . . . I owe it all to you.

The adviser is now in deep trouble and fears for his sanity, which is not too stable anyway. Nothing in nature is more pitiable than a joker confounded, and the adviser doesn't know whether he has been confounded or not. He may have invented a dazzling new method of trout fishing. Then again, he may be the victim of a joke, a horrifying thought to a joker.

This weekend he will be hurling heavy masses of a dozen nymphs, with three or four dangling loose, into every trout water he can find. He has got to get to the bottom of this in the only way he knows how or slip into the abyss of lunacy.

A Recipe for Quail Dish
That Will Prove
a Conversation Piece Later

Greenwood, South Carolina—It is painful to report before leaving quail country that the best quail dish encountered was not cooked according to an ancient plantation recipe of the Old South or the genius of a jolly old camp cook. It was cooked in a modern home under directions laid down in print by a beer outfit.

This dish could scarcely have been better. It follows the basic rule, restated forcibly in Raymond R. Camp's fine book, *Game Cookery,* that the cook must take pains to keep game from coming to the table dry. Nearly all game lacks natural fat.

This dish was prepared by Mrs. Charles Dickey, who got it from a booklet issued several years ago by the United States Brewers' Foundation in New York. I don't know where the beer people got it. The recipe can be adapted to grouse, chukar partridge, pheasant, and other birds.

There is nothing hard about cooking quail this way. This is the way to do it:

Fawn on some quail-hunting neighbor all summer long and begin hinting wistfully early in the fall that a few quail would be a better gift than a tax cut. Say that you have had no quail in many years and long to taste this peerless bird again before you die. Do anything to trick him into bringing you four quail.

Lock the doors against unexpected guests. Sprinkle the four quail, whole, with salt, pepper, and flour. Throw them in a hot skillet with a quarter of a cup of butter and brown them all over.

Pour half a cup of water into the skillet and toss in the slices of six large mushrooms or two seven-ounce cans of mushrooms. Cover the skillet and cook for ten minutes over low heat.

Now throw in two tablespoonfuls of chopped parsley and

75

cook ten more minutes. The quail ought to be tender by then, but if they are not cooked, cook them some more.

Turn off the fire. Serve the quail on buttered toast if you want to. In any case, eat them. Unlock the doors. Go somewhere and brag about it. Tell people you have friends who bring you all kinds of game, and talk preciously about how to cook it. Get some mileage out of the deal.

You might as well do that, because this dish is so much better than quail or any other game brought to the table dry and shriveled, or even just dry, that somebody might believe you.

To bring off the same thing with grouse or chukars, split the bird along the backbone and open it without tearing the breast. Quarter pheasants. Then do the same thing you did with the quail. Nothing to it.

There are those who will want to get fancy with this, and make it better talking material. This will be especially so when they have been able to harass friends into donating a dozen quail and thus are in a position to impress guests.

There is no harm in this. Go ahead and use white wine instead of water. It will sound better later in East Side bars and at church socials.

Get some wild rice, too, and then starve for a week or two to catch up financially. Serve cocktails ahead of the quail, brandy behind it, and wine with it. It is only money, and you've got quail.

If anybody wants to know more about this great dish, write to Mrs. Evelyn Dickey, R.F.D. 1, Greenwood, South Carolina. Don't write to me; I didn't cook it.

A Fellow Can Come Back
With a Bird or With a Passel
of Good Excuses

Colrain, Massachusetts—A boisterous wind following a furious rain mixed with a little snow is taking the last of the leaves off the trees now, stripping the proud upland hunter of one of his soundest excuses for not killing birds.

At first glance, it would seem that the grouse and pheasant hunter must now come home with game or come home silently. It is to laugh. An outdoorsman who can run out of valid, cogent reasons for not getting game is a sick-minded, resourceless knothead with no business hunting at all.

For example, the wet wind is tossing everything about now. Dogs can't work properly: the wind diffuses scent all over the landscape. Birds are wild and scary and flush far ahead of the gun. Grouse and pheasant fly downwind like bullets and crosswind like veering lightning. A hunter can make a triumph of one kill.

But suppose the wind drops dead. The dogs can't work properly: bird scent hangs close around the bird with no breeze to carry it out a little. Birds are wild and scary because they can see and hear long distances. Everything is still.

What if it gets cold? Dogs can't work properly because scent doesn't carry too well on cold air. Hunters get a little stiff and can't shoot so well. Birds are wild and scary because they have to move around too much because they need more feed.

But it could warm up, and that is no good. Dogs can't work properly: they get hot and panting, and scent doesn't carry too well on hot air. Birds get torpid and won't move much, but they are wild and scary because birds are wild and scary when it is hot.

It is too wet now, and dogs can't work properly in the heavy, humid air. Birds are wild and scary because they know they can't hear anything much on the soggy ground. Grouse are probably in the trees anyway, budding; and pheasant are sticking in the heavy brush.

But it will be too dry tomorrow or next day. Dogs won't be able to work properly because they need a little moisture in the air to get scent well. The birds will be wild and scary because they can hear man and dog moving in the leaves at long distances.

This year there is plenty of feed for grouse and pheasant. In fact, too much: feed is everywhere, and the birds can select their fare; they are therefore scattered and hard to locate. A man can't find a concentration, and dogs get discouraged.

Some years feed is scarce, and it is therefore hard to locate the birds. They are moving about too much, looking for something to eat, and may be concentrated on unlikely feed. Dogs get discouraged searching empty coverts.

Any of these conditions are sound reasons for missing birds when they do rise within range. Any of them explain why an otherwise perfect dog either runs wild or gives up and slinks along behind the master's heels. And either dog or master, or both, can be a little footsore, or off his feed, or bothered by a puffy eye, or, best of all, upset by a foolish companion hunter or dog.

Still, some of these things can be corrected after a day's hunt. The dog can't lie, but the master can always weight the truth a little for both of them, and he is no strong, hardy American outdoorsman who scorns to do it.

A Little Private Geometry
Can Turn Any Hunter
Into an Outdoorsman

Nothing is so valuable to the strong, hardy American outdoorsman as the private geometry by which he proves to himself that he has traveled long distances in the woods while cunningly keeping exact reckoning of his whereabouts.

The importance of this ability cannot be exaggerated, or even estimated. With it, a hunter who has traveled less than a mile can convince himself, and maybe others, that he has covered half of a Texas county. It works about like this:

Hunter leaves his car on a paved highway and walks westward, although he may not know it is westward, for a quarter of a mile in about an hour and a half, peering searchingly about all the while for a buck deer standing in the open and failing to see three other hunters doing the same thing.

Woods begin to look strange and forbidding after hunter has crossed three or four little rises of ground, which he will later describe as big, steep ridges. Hunter decides he better get back to his car because his lunch is there anyway. Hunter starts back, walking hastily, and reaches road half a mile from his car.

Now it is that half mile that is the key to his geometry. He cannot admit that he was only a quarter of a mile away from the car and still missed it by half a mile. He therefore calculates that, since he could not have missed his return direction by more than 5 degrees and the angle of return must therefore have been acute, he must have been six or seven miles in the woods when he turned back.

His story, then, runs somewhat like this:

"I kind of lost track of time and went futher'n I thought. Crossed five or six big ridges, cut around to the north to hit some beech woods on my way back, and finally came out no more'n couple hundred yards from the car. All that didn't git me nothing, though. Seen eight–ten does and one little spike horn, but nothin' worth shooting. Good country up there, though; didn't see no other hunters in twelve–fifteen miles of walking."

This is not a lie; it is private geometry, adorned by a little harmless fiction about living things to give it cohesion and movement. And the private geometry is based altogether on the acuteness of that angle of return.

This geometry, a separate and important branch of mathematics that would have fascinated Euclid if he had thought of it first, has deep social significance. It enables millions of Americans to regard themselves as well-dressed Hiawathas.

New York State has something like five hundred thousand deer hunters every year. Private geometry keeps 76.4 per cent of them hunting, according to weighted statistics weighted by the actuarial division of the American Institute of Outdoor Geometricians (est. 1960). Only 16.2 per cent (7.4 are either doubtful, independent, or inarticulate) would hunt if they had to walk where they said they had walked, or say they walked where they did walk.

But private geometry, the institute's analysts feel, is not used by hunters because they are hunters, but because they are people. Exactly the same geometry, it is believed, can be used and conceivably is used, in the computations of expense-account automobile mileage.

But whatever else its uses may be, private geometry is indispensable to the hunter. It is a branch of mathematics that ought to be investigated at Harvard or at Northeast Oklahoma Teachers College. A guided-missile agency that got a good grip on it might beat out all the other guided-missile agencies.

Modest Sharpshooter
Kills Two Quail While
Companions Miss Pheasants

Brighton, Illinois—A hunter got a surprise shot on two quail to-day, wheeled and waited for them to line up in a high wind, and dropped both of them dead.

There were other complications for him, too, such as the necessity of checking on the whereabouts of a couple of companions before he shot, but it is enough to say that the thing was just about perfect.

There is no special point in saying who this hunter was, but he was not Richard Wolters of Ossining, New York. Wolters was on another part of Nilo Farms, the game management research establishment of the Olin Mathieson Chemical Company, missing pheasants.

It is enough to say that the hunter that made this great shot, a man of almost painful modesty, is from New York City and observes the doings of hunters and fishermen.

There was some mystery tonight about what Wolters did to-day, and there was nothing certain about the conduct of Gene Brown of New York. Brown swore tonight on the innocent heads of his children that Wolters had not been observed to make a hit. Wolters made affidavit before a notary public that Brown made no hits.

They were hunting together and I cannot corroborate either of them. Their two companions, who are not notably silent men on any subject, had nothing to say on this one.

I was in the company of T. W. (Cotton) Pershall, manager of the Nilo Kennels, and a great dog trainer; Ed Kozicky, chief of the conservation department of Olin Mathieson; L. Rust Hills, Jr., of New York, who never had hunted before, and Bernard

81

White of New York, who had. Neither Pershall nor Kozicky shot.

Earlier in the day, I had been with Wolters in a blind at the bottom of a ravine to shoot mallards released a quarter of a mile away. Wolters, shooting a Winchester model 21 with a stock, the beautiful finish of which had been ruined by somebody's clumsy meddling, may have hit a duck in one of his nine shots; I can't be sure. He said he had. I got only a double in three shots, backing Wolters.

Pershall used a sturdy pointer and a young, vigorous setter this afternoon in the pheasant hunting. The two found, besides the two quail, a dozen pheasants and handled them beautifully. White took his shots as they came, and made everyone of them good.

Hills had bad luck. He killed a pheasant on his first shot at one and is not likely to amount to anything for the rest of his life. To make things worse, he downed a couple of others, and tonight was talking learnedly of game loads and reflecting aloud about what kind of guns he would acquire. He is a young man and might well have gone far.

Casting Expert
Makes the Easy Ones Look
Hard in Lake Ontario Display

Stony Island, Lake Ontario, New York—This night-fishing for largemouth black bass started out wrong last night because Alexander (Casey) Jones was afraid to fish with Joe Beamish. Knowing full well that a scared man doesn't fish well, Jones went with Mike Hudoba of Washington instead.

Jones was afraid to fish with Beamish for the following reason: he is executive editor the Syracuse *Herald-Journal* and Beamish is its hunting and fishing columnist.

82

The result was that Beamish night-fished with me. It was a painful experience.

Beamish is a grandstander. He makes easy catches look dazzling. Apparently desiring to intimidate me at the outset, he took out and rigged a tiny fly rod no more than five feet long and began to cast *sitting down.*

When you add to this the fact that we were in a rowboat, it becomes evident that Beamish was deliberately putting on a spectacular display. I had the feeling that it was a little vulgar.

It was nothing that he could cast a big, soft, hairy popping bug sixty feet with that little rod. That is not the point. And, anyway, pretty nearly anybody can do it with a little practice. It is simply ostentatious to use such a rod to throw a popping bug at all.

The fact that he took over my rod for a while and casually cast even bigger popping bugs even farther was nothing special, either. Just trying to impress with versatility. I could have cast that far if I had wanted to, but there is no need to cast great distances for bass.

All this went on before nightfall on the pond that runs up the middle of this island, within sight of Main Duck Island, where the late John Foster Dulles used to rest.

Our host, Frank Ash of Syracuse, who did not fish last night, had given instructions that we were to bring back three or four breakfast bass. I thought he was joking and didn't pay any particular attention, but Beamish took him seriously and started catching bass immediately. It still seems to me that that was a pretty solemn attitude.

He took a couple of two-pounders with his rod, then a couple with mine, then a couple with his. By this time it was getting dark, and Beamish switched to a spinning rod and popping plugs. He caught a couple more on that rig before the bass stopped striking for the evening. None of them weighed more than three pounds.

I forget how many I caught, but it couldn't have been over the limit because I was too busy not appreciating Beamish's performance. Showing off on your own water before visitors may be all right in some places, but not where I come from.

Meanwhile, Jones and Hudoba were trying to impress each

other, and succeeding fairly well. They stuck mostly to popping plugs, and claimed later to have caught and released six bass apiece. Probably they did; I wasn't able to break down either man's story or establish any clear contradiction by questioning them separately.

It does seem a little odd that they should both catch the same number of fish and that neither should have claimed to have caught the biggest fish.

And it might be considered slightly singular that, though both had heard Frank Ash order bass for breakfast, they released all of the fish they claimed to have caught. But probably they did catch six apiece; I have no proof to the contrary.

Well, it was a bad evening. Tomorrow I'm going to trick Jones and Beamish into fishing together.

Too Bad for Dick Wolters if He Puts His Betters to Shame Again Today

Bethel, Vermont—Sometimes it would pay a strong, hardy outdoorsman to stay indoors and read *The Rover Boys in the Green Mountains*. He can't break even, and justice dies the death of a dog.

Anybody ought to be able to kill grouse and woodcock around here, especially grouse. There are more grouse hereabouts than in any recent year. Warden Alton Blow, who has scratched his back against every tree in this region, says so, and he was the cicerone today.

The weather was clear and mild, and the autumn colors in the mountains were brilliant; everybody present described them in stupefying detail. Everything was right except that the woods were a little dry.

Grouse fluttered out on the road in front of the car on several occasions on the way to the hunting ground. They must have fluttered into hollow logs. In any case, grouse disappeared from humankind by the thousands. So did woodcock.

There is no accounting for this yet. Warden Blow probably will figure out later where the birds are and what they are feeding on. But nobody could figure it out today.

There are no beechnuts. The apple trees in the woods bear no apples. There are no thorn apples. Some grouse opened here in the last few days had clover in their craws, but we couldn't find any birds in the open.

Some hillsides are covered with barberries, but at camp apparently the grouse weren't feeding on barberries, or we couldn't find them there.

All this could be tolerated. But one or two things happened that a man can't live with.

John Falk's young setter put out two woodcock near me, but it happened that the new shell-vest I was wearing was a little tight, and an alder branch had just knocked my hat down over my eyes, and George Fremault was describing the color of a maple. In those circumstances no human could have hit those birds. Of course, I missed, but a strong, hardy outdoorsman never complains and never makes excuses.

Falk, who had downed two grouse and a woodcock in three shots yesterday, missed a grouse and stooped to the weak excuse that his safety had caught momentarily. Warden Blow missed a woodcock and said it was too far.

I jumped another grouse, but it ducked behind a spruce just as I pulled the trigger. I had just retied my boot and was a little out of breath anyway.

Then a grouse jumped, far from the dog, to the left of Dick Wolters of Ossining, New York. Wolters had never shot at a bird with a shotgun. Three years ago he shot six times at clay pigeons, missing them all, and that was his experience with a shotgun. He was along just for the walk.

This bird flew low through alders and across Wolters. He had no right to hit it. What happened was that he dumped it stone dead. Ten minutes later another jumped, again into the alders and this time on an upward slant. The ignorant Wolters dumped that one, too.

Falk and I were too courteous to pack up and go home, though it cannot be reasonably denied that the spectacle was revolting. Wolters, the apprentice seaman, now became a salty dog and soon was talking like an admiral. Warden Blow, exercising the authority of the sovereign State of Vermont, asked for my gun and Falk's and wouldn't give them back.

Thus ended a bad day. Wolters will miss tomorrow, or somebody else will hit, or we will commiserate with the Widow Wolters.

Dark Glasses Overboard
Help a Marlin Escape—
Dark Glances Aboard Ensue

Hatteras, North Carolina—This fishing for blue marlin off Cape Hatteras, especially in a tournament, is a complicated business, but a man of resolution can beat it if he tries. The thing to do is take everybody's advice.

Things were going along pretty well in the first International Blue Marlin Tournament, sponsored by the Hatteras Marlin Club, yesterday, when I decided to step in and win it. It was well worth winning by that time, with a dozen big blues already caught and a couple of score hooked and lost.

I would have won it, too, if James French Baldwin, of Locust Valley, Long Island, hadn't distracted me by throwing his dark glasses overboard. Baldwin was my host aboard his cruiser *Marlina*. He has fished all over the East Coast and in the Bahamas for billfish and is sometimes called Spiderweb Baldwin for his unbreakable addiction to light tackle.

Baldwin put me on the right outrigger with fifteen-thread line, the only stuff he had aboard. The seas were fairly heavy but regular. After a while some kind of billfish—so the captain,

Dick Jarmack, said—took my bait while it was being dropped back. In a couple of minutes the hook pulled free.

Baldwin muttered something to the effect that I hadn't done everything wrong, by which he clearly meant that I had done everything right.

A white marlin came next and lost the hook on the first jump. The mate, George Clermont, said I hadn't dropped back enough. Baldwin said I had dropped back too much.

A woman who was hanging around on the *Marlina* said I hadn't dropped back at all. As a matter of fact, I had dropped back just right, but I wasn't out there to catch white marlin and didn't try very hard.

At 2:30 P.M., just before the tournament ended, a huge blue marlin took my bait and made off with it, breaking the sound barrier. This was a fish that would have won the tournament.

Baldwin said it weighed four hundred and fifty pounds, but he was in the cockpit and couldn't see it as well as Jarmack in the Texas Tower. Jarmack said it weighed over five hundred, but fishing captains, accustomed to running rough inlets and stuff like that, are trained in caution.

It is conservative to say that the fish weighed upward of nine hundred pounds, which would have beaten Esteban Bird of San Juan, Puerto Rico, who later won the tournament with 881 pounds of fish.

Anyway, the fish tried to circle the boat, turned back, turned again, leaping and thrashing all the way. Jarmack had to turn the *Marlina* and run her at high speed to get a double belly out of the line.

But I would have caught the fish all right, if Baldwin hadn't thrown those dark glasses overboard. I got to wondering why he had done it and forgot about the fish.

A man ought not to do a thing like that when somebody is fighting a tournament-winning fish. Anyway, I absently let the line become tight too fast, and it parted.

Baldwin was calm through all this. Scarcely screamed at all, very much. The reason he threw those glasses overboard was that he just didn't like them any more, he said later, and decided to buy something else.

87

Or the Sad but True Tale
of the One (One Rod
and Reel) That Got Away

St. Petersburg, Florida—A striking king mackerel snatched rod
and reel from the hands of an angler aboard the *Little Jewel* in
the Gulf of Mexico today, but it wasn't the angler's fault. Somebody had just pointed out a twelve-foot manta ray to him, and
he was busy admiring it.

Anyway, at the moment strikes weren't so frequent as they
had been earlier and would be soon again, and, besides that, the
angler was expertly eating a sandwich, smoking a cigarette, and
drinking hot coffee. Who can keep a rod secure in those circumstances?

This happened ten miles out in the Gulf while three anglers
were catching fifty-six king mackerel weighing from three to ten
pounds apiece. This sort of fishing can cause a man to relax his
vigilance.

A. B. (Bev) Nabers had driven his fast cruiser there after
Captain Rex Cole, Jr., had caught three or four gallons (or
pecks or something) of white minnows under a bridge with four
throws of a cast net. Cole, himself a charter captain with his own
boat as well, was along just to relax.

Some fifty boats were clustered out there near a buoy. Many
were outboarders. What a sudden, violent squall, common in
the Gulf, might have done to them is hard to think about.

None of them were taking fish to any extent when we arrived.
Nabers and Cole said the king fish were there, but had not yet
come up. We trolled deep-running plugs for a few minutes and
caught three or four that way before a king hit a minnow Cole
was dangling a few feet behind the *Little Jewel*.

That was the signal that the fish were up, and the carnage
began. Two spinning rods and a bait-casting rod carrying an

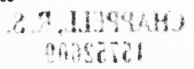

Ambassadeur salt-water reel were put in use, all with minnows from an anchored boat.

For a while the kings wouldn't allow a minnow to get settled in the water before they struck. Repeatedly, three fish were in play at once. Most were small at first—maybe three pounds each.

After a while things slacked a little: fish were striking only every three or four minutes. It was natural enough for one of the fishermen to turn to a sandwich and coffee, which often brings on a cigarette. Nabers chose that moment to point out that giant manta, which must have weighed a ton and was straddling along just under the surface.

Well, the king struck and the rod went overboard forever. Nobody could be blamed for it, reasonably. Nabers said something to the effect that a man ought to know his limitations and not try to eat, smoke, fish, and drink coffee simultaneously, by which he plainly meant that if it hadn't been for the coffee the rod wouldn't have been lost.

This was clear recognition that I could have handled the sandwich, the cigarette, and the fish while watching the manta, and it was generous of Nabers to state it that way. Cole didn't say anything except to note politely that I had not dropped the sandwich.

Some Methods for Getting Up at 5 A.M. to Go Deer Hunting, but Why Bother?

Colrain, Massachusetts—There are two major schools of thought about how to get up at 5 A.M. to go deer hunting. Neither of them concerns the insufferable fellow who leaps impatiently from his bed to greet the dawn with a glad shout.

This man is not to be considered as a hunting companion or

any other kind of companion anyway. He is almost certain to take cold showers, watch his diet, deliberately take exercise, be cheerful, and talk about all of these accomplishments all day long.

Of the two major schools, the first is composed of those who set their clocks ahead and their alarms back, thus deluding themselves into thinking they are getting up at 6 A.M. This is workable, but dishonorable. Such a man starts the day as both the swindler and the swindled. This is immoral: a man should either hunt with the hounds or run with the hare.

The second school is made up of men who deputize a member of the family to get them up at 5 A.M. by offers of reward and threats of penalty. This is sound practice: honest, straightforward, and efficient. It promotes family discipline. It encourages others to rise early and catch worms. There is no delusion, no subterfuge.

There is a third and even larger school, but its system is archaic. Members of this group simply turn the alarm off at 5 A.M. with the mental excuse that it probably is raining hard. This method works pretty well. The hunter gets a couple of hours extra sleep and ordinarily does not inconvenience any more than a half-dozen other people, including those with whom he was to have hunted. But it simply is not modern or progressive. Daniel Boone used it. The Democrats were still using it in November.

Somebody was using the wrong system this morning, since we didn't get started until 8:30. On second thought, maybe it was the right system for today. For the second day in a row, the fog was about as thick as a radio jollyboy's twaddle.

Fresh deer tracks were plentiful enough, but so were ways to get lost, or at least confused, in strange woods. I selected this day to forget both compass and watch, though I was thoughtful enough to bring a shotgun.

On one occasion today, while hunting in a big batch of pines cut by little ridges and ravines running in every direction, I heard the sound of barnyard geese, which I assumed belonged to a farm that was supposed to be dead south of me. I was headed for that farm, and used the geese for my compass.

This was a brilliant piece of woodcraft, except that the geese resided on another farm to the west. The mistake was discovered when a big roaring brook appeared where no big roaring brook should have been. But by that time, considerably more pine woods had been covered than were on the schedule, and I was a mile out of place.

There were a lot of fresh deer tracks in the snow under those pines, but, if any deer were jumped, they were driven west instead of south toward my colleagues. My colleagues were two in number and we were trying to cover the entire side of a long ridge. It was like three men trying to canvass the Empire State Building in a morning.

But the day was no total loss. Billy Pratt of Bernardston, crossing a pasture with Francis Hafey of Whately, jumped a deer just at dusk on the edge of the woods. It was still lawful to shoot, but the deer was too quick for them. Yet it was clear profit: this was Billy's fifteenth birthday, he had a new 16-gauge pump gun and his first hunting license, having just passed the National Rifle Association's safety course. He had sworn to see a deer today or bust something, not his new gun. Thus was avoided a painful injury.

That ended the business of the day except for a ten-mile drive on narrow roads, which took just over an hour in the thick fog.

There is a lot to be said for that third school of 5 A.M. rising, but the method ought to be improved and extended. If a strong, hardy outdoorsman played his cards just right, he could stay in bed all day.

It's True That Yanks Beat
Confederates, but Not, Apparently,
on Shooting Skill

Belhaven, North Carolina—John Jefferson, a Confederate to the death, found out at length today why the Confederates lost: the Yankees could not shoot, but starved them out.

He thought he discovered the reason, anyway. He thought he discovered it in the person of Richard Wolters of Ossining, New York.

Jefferson is an honest and conscientious guide for River Forest Manor, a hangout for goose shooters and quail hunters. The War Between the States is far behind him and his family, but he does keep his senses. Wolters, art director of *Business Week,* is a native Philadelphian and a chemistry graduate of Penn State. The city of Philadelphia was threatened in some way by Lee before the Battle of Gettysburg. So Wolters and Jefferson have something in common, whatever it may be.

Jefferson was Wolters' guide today for both geese and quail. It may be said mercifully in the beginning that Wolters and Jefferson got no geese and only two quail; and that on these facts Jefferson has at last soothed his mind about that bad old war of a century ago.

In the morning, everybody at Axson Smith's River Forest Manor went after geese. That means going into corn and soybean fields and waiting in fence-row blinds for geese to come off Lake Mattamuskeet on their way to feed. A good cross-section of the story is soon told:

Four Yankees got a goose apiece in blinds a couple of miles from the lake: Robert Rose of Harrison, New York; Gene Hill of Blairstown, New Jersey; John Falk of White Plains, New York, and James Rikhoff of Princeton, New Jersey.

It turned out later that each of them got his second goose in the afternoon. In fact, the geese came in to their decoys so ferociously that they might have shot five limits. But success is a bore.

Jefferson had managed to get Wolters only a couple of shots at geese in the morning. Wolters had missed them both, one because a two-by-four had got caught in his eyelash, the other because a basketball had got caught in his throat.

In the afternoon, Jefferson took Wolters quail hunting with Wolters' fine setter, Beau. Jefferson said later that Beau was as good a bird dog in his first year as a man could ever hope to see with that kind of owner. He said the dog was brilliantly intelligent and perfectly tractable. He said the dog had a spectacularly sensitive nose.

He said the dog had everything, nearly. It was unfortunate, he said, that things had happened as they did.

Let us not make a dramatic thing of this, it is only a matter of dog training. It is easy enough to say, on Jefferson's word, that the dog found two big coveys and two small coveys, and that the dog followed out singles faithfully and truly. It is enough to say that two dead quail were picked up from the ground. There is still some dispute over how many shells Wolters fired.

There's no dispute that Beau is a great dog for a first-year dog. The debate is over other issues. But Jefferson is at last satisfied and at peace: the Yankees could never do it again.

An Angler Can't Relax
Even When Fish Don't Bite:
He's Got to Watch Guide

Loon Bay, New Brunswick—The St. Croix River is at a low
stage now and very clear. Bass fishing is generally poor, but the
visiting angler cannot relax because it is essential at such a time
to keep a close eye on his guide.

That is particularly so if the guide is Fred Brisley, a man who
will stoop to carrying worms secretly in his pocket. Guides hate
to be outfished and are apt to turn tricky if it happens. Brisley
has already turned tricky on me, but George Welock, operator
of Loon Bay Lodge and Brisley's boss, warned me in advance,
and I am watching him.

Welock told me that Brisley was fishing a New York dude last
month and they locked horns in a bitter battle. The dude was
outfishing Brisley at the rate of about five to four when suddenly
the tide of battle turned and Brisley caught five bass while the
dude was catching nothing.

This dude was a grim loser, as all fierce competitors are, and for three hours he wouldn't speak to Brisley. Finally he made a cast and caught Brisley's line. When he brought in his own spinning lure to clear it, Brisley's came with it. Attached to each of the three hooks was a large, lively night crawler.

After the proper amount of yowling, the dude said, "All bets are off and you got to give me some of them worms."

Welock says the dude thought the thing over and went back to Loon Bay Lodge as happy as could be. He allowed it was more fun to catch Brisley cheating than to catch twenty small-mouth bass. But, for the rest of his stay here, he fished facing the stern of the canoe, thus robbing Brisley of his unfair advantage.

Last night I saw a gleam of a flashlight outdoors, and the explanation of it leaped to mind instantly. Easing around the back of the house, I caught Brisley picking up night crawlers on the lawn. But you can't put a guide out of countenance. He had the brass to tell me that he was catching those night crawlers for a couple of little nieces of his who wanted to go fishing today. And he knows that I know that he hasn't got any nieces.

Well, I forgot to sit facing Brisley today when we went bass fishing in the St. Croix below Loon Bay Lodge. The fish weren't moving very much, and for a long time I didn't catch anything except a small bass and three good-sized pickerel. Couldn't get anything much started on either popping bugs or surface plugs.

Brisley was fishing the fly rod with popping bugs all this time, and talking cheerfully. That should have made me suspicious, but I am the trusting type, never suspecting a thing until I feel the knife between my shoulder blades.

It doesn't pay to be that way. Brisley finally hooked a bass weighing about three pounds and worked it into the boat. I offered to net it for him, but he said no, it wouldn't be any trouble at all to do it himself. He got the net before I could reach it.

I can't prove even now that Brisley was using a worm. But the circumstantial evidence is powerful. Brisley brought the fish near the stern of the boat and nearly broke his back twisting around to net it where I couldn't see him do it.

Moreover, he stayed in that awkward position for three or four minutes while he got the hook out and released the bass.

Then he stayed that way a little longer doing something that I couldn't see.

And when he finally did turn around, I saw that he had secretly changed from a popping bug to a streamer. Worms don't work at all on popping bugs, but they do fine on streamers. Of course, there was no worm on the streamer by that time. Obviously he had taken it off while freeing the fish.

I didn't come up here to watch guides all day and try to block their vain tricks. Tomorrow I am going to search Brisley before we get into the canoe. And I am not going to let him search me.

Our Man Is Too Polite
to Shoot a Deer That
Won't Take Its Hat Off

Colrain, Massachusetts—Deer hunting sometimes seems like seeking a two-headed man wearing a Homburg and a carnival cap on Broadway during New Year's Eve. There are probably twenty of them, but you can't find them. Those Homburgs are protective coloration.

That is about the way it was on this mountain today. There were deer all over the place, but they might as well have been wearing a Homburg; they were visible to everybody but me. Yet that is the way to have it. The trick is to get the deer on the last day of hunting.

Before it was fully light, Joe Jurek, a Colrain orchardist, was shooting at deer within two hundred yards of where I walked with Louis Pratt, a Bernardston cattle dealer who would rather race horses than trade cattle and would rather hunt deer than race horses.

Probably we jumped the two deer and sent them to Jurek, although we didn't see them jump. Anyway, the shot was too long for Jurek, and nothing came of it.

Less than an hour later, Francis Hafey, a Whately farmer, pushed two bucks out of a beech grove toward Pratt, whose gun misfired. Pratt was just west of me, but those deer didn't turn west; they were silly enough to turn east and in about one minute were dead. They had separated, and each had run directly to a standing hunter.

This was a freezing day after a day of thawing, which meant a stiff and noisy crust of snow. It was an ideal day for standing; you could hear a deer coming for half a mile. So we walked.

At the end of one of these drives, Joe and Bill Jurek, Pratt, and Hafey met in a hollow between two knobs at the top of the mountain and sat down to smoke and talk. I was approaching them when a deer ambled down one of the knobs toward me, turned in their direction, and galloped across open pasture about fifty yards from them.

Hafey waited for the Jureks to fire, and the Jureks, thinking about Pratt's earlier misfire, waited for him. Finally, but a bit too late, all of them pulled trigger. It didn't do Pratt any good; his gun misfired again. Didn't do the others any good, either.

Pratt ran as hard as he could over a little ridge, caught sight of the deer again and tried once more. The gun fired, which astonished him so much that he missed. He pulled the trigger again, just for laughs, and it fired again. Tonight he gave the gun to a fellow who once swindled him in a cow trade.

Lawrence Shearer, Jr., of Colrain got a long shot at that deer, too, but he will be hunting again tomorrow. Shearer had already jumped a buck but hadn't got a shot at him. The Jureks had both jumped deer without getting a shot. Everybody was jumping deer, except one hunter who was waiting for the last day.

In the afternoon three of us took stands while three drove a hillside covered with pine and hardwood. Hafey was sent to cover a barway in a fence on the wood's edge. He had never been there before and he covered the wrong barway. The driver sent a fine buck through the barway he should have covered.

Shearer, following that buck later, jumped it within two hundred yards of a stand I was covering just ahead of him. But it cut around a knoll and headed for Opelika, Alabama. Shearer doesn't know anybody in Opelika, so he stuck around.

No more deer appeared. Tomorrow is slated to be cold and

sleety, a hard day for hunting. As likely as not, everybody will get a deer. Pratt will be using another gun.

Senate Subcommittee Will Get Report on Unethical Practices of Deer

Colrain, Massachusetts—It turned out today that the deer in a certain section of this vicinity were guilty of unethical practices, as defined by the McClellan subcommittee.

This was unfortunate for western Massachusetts, a region that has so far escaped the attention of the subcommittee, which is investigating for the Senate the doings of both management and labor.

The subcommittee is sure to hear about it because Diana Hirsh of New York, a special literary consultant to the subcommittee, who collaborates on writing its reports, was a witness to the proceedings. In addition to her professional faculties, she is suspicious by nature and not inclined to forgive or condone weakness or error.

She had been told that this batch of real estate abounded in deer, and did not believe it. Consultants to Senate committees do not believe things anyway. But Miss Hirsh's intellect is broadgauged: she was willing to accept proof if the proof was somewhat better than Jimmy Hoffa's.

The mountain on which we were hunting had been alive with deer a couple of days ago. They had paraded up and down and along the ridges, all of them big deer, and their tracks proved it.

Louis Pratt of Bernardston, Massachusetts, and I took long swings around the north end of the mountain and found one big track after another. But all of them were a couple of days old, as the crusty snow showed too plainly.

We were trying to drive deer to Miss Hirsh and a woman of

a certain age, a matronly type, whom we had stationed in a strategic spot near an old sugar house at the edge of a beech grove.

That was the unfortunate part of it. Miss Hirsh had simplified deer hunting, which she had never tried before, as a shrewd committee counsel, say Robert Kennedy, might simplify it: either there were deer around here or there were not.

There were not. No deer appeared before Miss Hirsh or the woman of a certain age. It availed nothing for Pratt and me to point out that big deer had been all over the territory only a day or so ago, leaving their signatures in the stiff snow. Miss Hirsh pointed out coldly that she and the woman of a certain age had seen no deer.

It was bootless for us to recount that we had followed the track of a big wounded buck through the beech grove just below us, into an alder swamp in a brook bottom, across a couple of sheep pastures, and onto a hardwood knoll. Miss Hirsh pointed out coldly that neither she nor the woman of an uncertain age had seen any deer.

This region is in bad with Washington. Miss Hirsh's report to the committee will be rigidly factual—fair, just, and candid, but not warm, not friendly. It is fortunate that Massachusetts has a Democratic Senator and a Republican Senator, and that their relations seemed to be uncommonly cordial for men of opposite parties. Neither of them has been publicized as a deer hunter, which may also be lucky for Colrain in this case.

Pratt and I wound up the day exhausted from our effort to save this region from the terrors of senatorial scrutiny. Miss Hirsh and the other woman, who had sat comfortably for hours on chair cushions carried to their ridge, and who had treated themselves to a fire for an hour or so, came out of the woods fresh and sarcastic.

Miss Hirsh pointed out coldly that, while she had heard great claims and had listened to plenty of unsupported assertions, she still had not seen a deer. She could hardly see her way clear to make a favorable report to the committee.

How to Stay Alive
in Woods: See the Other Hunter
Before He Sees You

Every year and all year long a great deal is written about how to avoid shooting somebody in the woods, and for that matter there never can be too much of that sort of propaganda. But what about the business of dodging the fire of other hunters?

There are two sides to this coin. How to remain a nonkiller is important; but how to stay alive counts, too.

In Eastern deer and pheasant shooting, particularly, this is a matter worthy of the attention of the uninsured. Pheasant hunters gather in good game areas like gulls around a garbage boat. Some of them spray the air vigorously with birdshot whenever a feather moves. Makes you think.

Deer hunters skulk numerously in good woods, armed with rifles and shotguns, and some of them are as nervous as race horses. A hunter ought to consider these matters this year especially, when New York has a one-day doe season in thirty-two counties. Nobody has to look for horns on that day, and some may shoot at anything that moves or makes noise.

In the last few years I have talked to thirteen hundred and sixty-four deer hunters about how to stay alive in the woods. Many of their answers were long and categorical, and some were incoherent. All efforts to get this fascinating and vital stuff punched out on cards for analysis by thinking machines have failed; statisticians and thinking-machine people distrust figures of less than nine digits.

Yet the answers are easy to analyze. The one common factor in all of them is the basic thought: see the other hunter before he sees you. That gives you the drop on him. You can (1) hide (2) run away (3) whistle or sing to prove you are not a deer, or (4) in extreme cases, and not to be recommended for anybody not wearing a badge, shoot him first.

There are other ways, of course. You can whistle or sing all the time. Or sit on the ground in the corner of a stone wall. Or buy ten thousand acres, hire patrols, and permit nobody else to hunt or trespass. Or sit in your car on a logging road.

The last method is not recommended. A few years ago a hunter in Vermont, seeing what he thought was a deer protruding above the laurel, tore the top off his own tan convertible with a 12-gauge shotgun. Still, it's warm in a heated car.

But the best thing is to see the other man first. This is a simple but not easy thing to do. You look. It is necessary to look at not only the general shape of the landscape but at some of the things on it, especially things that are not moving. Other hunters can sometimes sit still for as long as six minutes and say they sat still for two hours.

Move slowly and keep looking at everything. If you can see the other man first, you can take one of the precautions mentioned above. If he sees you first, he may think you saw him first and shoot you in self-protection. Or he may take you for a moose, particularly if you are wearing scarlet from head to foot and weigh no more than a hundred and forty pounds.

Never assume that the other man has passed the hunter safety course provided by the state, or that he has ever had firearms in his hands before, or that he has ever seen a deer. Maybe he has never even seen another man. See him first.

A few years ago I came out of the woods into a western Massachusetts hillside pasture and saw a man watching an orchard at the edge of the woods. He could have seen me by turning his eyes 15 degrees.

But he didn't see me as I walked parallel to his line of vision, in open pasture, and it made me uneasy. I changed course to get behind him. Still he didn't move his head. At length I was directly behind him, maybe a hundred feet away. His oblivious manner was frightening. It seemed to me that this was a man who might whirl and fire at a movement or sound.

I whistled, and he didn't move. That scared me doubly. I stretched out on the ground and whistled piercingly. He turned.

"Whyn't you keep quiet?" he snarled. "I might of thought you was a deer and shot you, except I seen you."

That was a lie. He never had a chance, because I seen him.

Boy Toad Merchant Shows
Why Grown Men Won't
Dig Their Own Worms

This boy Paul lives in New Jersey, and his profession explains why grown men can make a fine living raising and selling fishing worms to people fully able to dig them. Paul is a toad merchant.

The story comes from Bob O'Byrne of New York, who is Paul's uncle. He tells it this way:

Paul was going into church one Sunday morning with his mother when she noticed a clumsy bulge in his pants pocket. She asked him what he had in there. Paul stalled. She insisted; said he couldn't go into church with his pockets bulging that way.

Paul offered not to go to church, but she declined this generous offer without thanks. In the end came the imperious command: "Now-what-have-you-got-in-those-pockets, young man?"

Paul is a boy who knows when his luck has run out. He said dutifully that he didn't have nothing in there but a couple lousy little ol' toads. Using threats and coercion, his mother caused him to liberate these animals. Then, his cup of sorrow running over, Paul uttered their valedictory:

"Aw, gee, and they was both FORTY CENTERS!"

Even a woman must investigate a crack like that from a boy. After church, Paul's mother put him on the grill. Dispirited after an exceptionally dull sermon, he gave up easily and told all.

Paul caught toads and sold them to a pet shop. Little toads brought twenty cents, big toads brought forty cents. Paul was doing a thriving business. O'Byrne said he even had two smaller boys working for him at fifteen cents a small toad and thirty cents a big toad, but he may have been just bragging about his nephew. Anyway, the kid was a prime contractor, whether he had any subcontractors or not.

But who bought those toads from the pet shop? Why, other boys bought those toads from the pet shop, for pets. The shop sold them for a mark-up that O'Byrne thought was about a dime.

How come boys are buying toads for pets instead of catching their own? Well, that is the way things are nowadays: boys still like to play with toads, but have lost their ability or willingness to catch their own. Boys have allowances to cover all needs now, even toads. That puts Paul in business as a toad merchant.

What is he going to do with the dough he makes peddling toads? Why, probably, he will save some of it until next spring and buy worms to go fishing. Or maybe he will buy grasshoppers.

That explains in full this worm business that has been bothering me for several years. Some worm ranchers raise hundreds of thousands of worms every year, and I never could figure out who could be buying them all. There just never did seem to be that many fishermen.

It is plain enough now. Those worms are bought by the fathers of the boys who buy Paul's toads.

The Tale of an Elusive
Cottontail and a "Hunting"
Dog That Turned Tail

Colrain, Massachusetts—There is a dog around that is going to get his lumps some day and I hope to be around to see it.

This animal is a big, black, glossy, ungainly house dog, but he thinks he is a hunting dog, a conviction for which there is not the least excuse. His name is Kelly, but he is widely known as Stupid, and with good reason. He is not my dog and I can talk about him without embarrassment; to name the owner would be sadistic.

People are training hunting dogs around here now. Stupid joins all hunting parties cordially and proceeds to disorganize everything, including the landscape.

He has nose enough to detect a pheasant and will flush it ahead of the hunting dogs with a joyous leap. He jumps playfully at dogs on stand, pesters their owners with vigorous affection, and cannot be driven away.

Stupid reminds me strongly of a poodle named Evelyn, owned

by an English boy who lived for a while near me many years ago. Evelyn used to act about the same way and patently thought she was a great hunter.

One day, Evelyn, Ernest the English boy, and I were at the edge of an old rice field by a railroad track when a rabbit darted in front of Evelyn. She bounded after it with shrill cries of excitement. It was the first rabbit she had ever seen.

The grass was high in that field, and Evelyn soon lost sight of the rabbit. Her way of dealing with this trouble was to leap high above the grass about every ten feet and look around wildly.

The rabbit ran in loops and doubles, and Evelyn raced without any plan at all, shrilling all the while. This apparently confused the cottontail because he, too, soon began to leap above the grass in attempts to locate Evelyn. I have never since seen a rabbit do that.

Their leaps were so synchronized that both were never in the air simultaneously. As the rabbit came down from a high jump, Evelyn would shoot upward. Then the rabbit, then Evelyn, then the rabbit, then Evelyn. The English boy and I, standing on a pile of ties, began to get seasick.

Finally, the inevitable happened. Evelyn and the rabbit shot into the air at the same time, facing each other at a distance of not more than two feet.

It was a soul-searing experience for Evelyn. She twisted in the air, came down facing the opposite direction, and set sail for home with hysterical yelps. Her piteous squalling could be heard five minutes later when she was a mile away.

That cured Evelyn. She could not be coaxed into the country again with any blandishments whatever. Nobody wanted to, anyway.

Something of the sort is bound to happen to Stupid sooner or later. It would be a privilege, a boon beyond value, to be present when it happens.

But a man can't count on seeing a thing like that. Probably I won't be anywhere around when an enraged field mouse makes a jump at Stupid and drives him forever from the field. A more somber thought is that maybe it will never happen, and Stupid will keep right on lolloping around hunting parties forever, flushing every bird within miles, and ruining hunting dogs with his tries to smother their owners with elephantine caresses.

Still, maybe that wouldn't be so bad. Hunting dogs are too serious anyway, though not half so serious as their owners.

Hunter Who Misses Deer at Ten Yards Bears Watching by His Friends

Colrain, Massachusetts—It is a sad duty to report that Joe Jurek missed a deer today at ten yards with a 20-gauge slug, but it is an ill thing to conceal the truth, and nobody outside television ever gains anything by it.

The rough part of it is that Jurek is not cooperating. Far from dredging up some sound excuses for missing, as strong, hardy, self-respecting outdoorsmen almost always do, Jurek only grunts. Once, under the intolerable needling of his son, Jim, he did condescend to growl:

"Damn if I know why I missed the little cuss."

There is the shadow of an implied excuse in that sentence. The deer was *very small*. I saw it, and it might even be said, by stretching the truth mercilessly, that I missed it myself. Yet Jurek missed it at ten yards, and he wouldn't miss a snowshoe rabbit at that range.

In sober truth, this is revolutionary. I have seen Jurek kill an eight-point buck stone dead with that same 20-gauge shotgun at one hundred and eighty yards—I paced it off myself. This happened several years ago within sight of where he missed that little cuss today.

The hundred-end-eighty-yard shot was an accident—he was trying to turn a running deer toward Lawrence Shearer, fired fifteen or twenty feet above and ahead of it, and chanced to strike it directly on the backbone.

I have also been close by when he shot deer with that 20-gauge at fifty or sixty yards, and with a rifle in Vermont at twenty yards and one hundred yards. Jurek is a good deer shot, besides being able to guess what a deer will do in most circumstances.

He guessed it right today. His son Jim and Lawrence Shearer, Jr., both young Colrain men, and Francis Hafey of Whately, Massachusetts, were going through a neck of woods in the hope of driving deer out to Jurek and me. We were under a wide powerline running steeply uphill through Jurek's pasture and wood lot.

Jurek had chosen the upper stand for himself, and I took the lower. He was about a hundred yards above me, but I thought he was a couple of ledges higher, maybe two hundred and fifty yards away. When the three drivers jumped the deer, the animals ran directly to Jurek, as deer almost always do.

I didn't know he was in their path and shot twice at the first one as it crossed the powerline a hundred yards above me on the jump. The idea was to turn it toward where I thought Jurek was, or downhill toward me.

Well, it might be said I missed the deer, since I didn't hit it, but that would be mere quibbling, legal straw-splitting, trivial semantics, malicious exaggeration. Besides, I was cold and shivering, and not even Annie Oakley could shoot while shivering.

I don't know whether Jurek was shivering or not. But he did miss that deer four times while it was running toward him and once as it was going by, and then he missed its companion, also a very small deer, going away.

Junior Shearer missed one of them once, too. Shearer has seen every deer anyone else among us has seen this week, and a few that he, alone, saw. He has been busy breaking woods-traveling records all the time and he actually jumped these deer today at the end of a 3:52.7 mile uphill through stony pasture and hardwood.

After jumping the deer and not getting an immediate shot, Shearer ran a hundred yards to the powerline, also uphill, in 0:09.1 and got his shot downhill at a hundred and fifty yards.

But the hundred-yard run was done over open ground, and

he was wearing his light rubber boots, not his insulated boots, so the time was a little slow for Shearer in the woods. Both Jureks say that Shearer cannot outrun his great-grandmother on pavement or a level dirt track.

He missed the deer.

That was the action for today. No amount of shacking through woods could get another deer started. Joe Jurek is being watched carefully tonight, though he is not the kind of man to do himself harm deliberately.

Search for Solitude Takes
Hunter From Massachusetts
Woods to New York

A hunter from western Massachusetts made the agonizing decision yesterday, after forty-eight hours of prayerful thought, to move to New York City and never to set foot in the woods again.

It is not that he loves New York but that it is the only place he knows where a human can have absolute and soothing solitude. The woods, he said, are now thickly populated by a race of compulsive babblers, and nobody can evade their company.

His decision came after a final, shattering day of deer hunting. It was Saturday, the last day of Massachusetts deer hunting and a day off for most of the working population of his region. The woods were full of hunters, but most of them were not hunting; they were associating closely and cordially with anybody they could find.

This man (call him Jones) began the day with six companions on a drive in Leyden. Jones's stand was beside a brook. As is his custom in these circumstances, he crouched motionless in good cover, between a huge maple and a boulder. Even a crow would have had trouble locating him. But a hunter, not a member of his party, found him and opened a lively conversation.

Jones told him politely that a drive was in progress, and even invited him to take a stand somewhere nearby. But the man chatted on like a hermit freed of a vow of silence after twenty years. The drivers came out, reporting that they had driven four deer toward that stand but that the deer had turned at the sound of voices.

Jones is a magnanimous type and he said he understood why this man, whom he knew, could not stop talking. He said the man was a fiercely ardent character: he dearly loved not to spend money. He said the man had early developed the stratagem of talking relentlessly to avoid the subject of payment, and now could not stop. Jones prepared philosophically for the next drive.

This time he was posted at the top of a pasture surrounded on three sides by woods. He was alone. He concealed himself again. A strange hunter promptly sought him out and began an anecdote. Jones finally got rid of him.

Two more hunters appeared in the pasture three hundred yards away and Jones stood up so that they could see and avoid him. They marched directly to him and asked him wittily how many deer he had killed. Jones said there was a drive on. One of them replied, with no signs of moving on, that there were plenty of deer around. Jones said the drive was coming from the east and that if any deer were ahead of the drivers they should be out any minute. The hunter replied enthusiastically that there were plenty of deer around, all right.

After ten minutes they took off—to the east, in the direction of the drive. This completed the foul-up of Jones's stand, but he was not through. The first hunter who had appeared came back again and talked until Jones left. Jones found a field of hardhack nearby and sat down out of sight in it to brood until the drive was over.

Late in the afternoon Jones was sitting beside a little dry swamp in hardwood at the edge of a large pasture. It was the last hour of the hunting season and he thought that he had found a spot unknown to man.

A teen-age boy walked within ten feet of him, swashing

leaves louder than a thousand gray squirrels. A hunter walked down from behind him and started to cross the swamp in front of him. Jones whistled softly to give notice of his presence. The hunter looked up, saw him, and continued to cross his stand. Jones whistled piercingly. The hunter stopped again, looked again, and continued.

The stand was dead for at least ten minutes, so Jones smoked. Twenty minutes later, when the sun was down and the swamp beginning to get dusky, he heard a deer just below him and to the left. He listened for ten minutes as his deer, confused by the many hunters about, made little nervous circles and stopped to listen and sample the breeze.

Finally, Jones could see it, but not well enough to identify it positively as a deer and not a stray Jersey heifer. It was moving slowly toward him. At this moment the teen-ager returned, swashing leaves again, and the deer took off with flag bobbing.

The boy asked Jones cordially whether he had seen any deer. Almost in the same breath he said excitedly that he had just heard one jump. Jones stood up silently and walked away into the dusk, a beaten man.

Trout-Fishing Pandoras
Will Observe
Tackle-Box Ritual Today

This is the Sunday dedicated to getting ready for the opening of the trout season next Saturday. Here is the ritual to be followed:

Get the fly rod out, find a loose guide, try to fix it, and take it up to a tackle shop tomorrow. If you don't know how to fix a loose guide, nobody can tell you. If you do know how, why are you reading this?

Take the fly reel apart, put it back together, and go to a

tackle shop tomorrow and find out what to do with the part left over.

Take the line off the fly reel and try to clean off the dirt and salt water that have been on it since last fall. Stretch it to get out the kinks that have been in it all winter. That won't work, but do it anyhow, it's part of the ceremony. Then go to a tackle shop tomorrow and get a new line.

Paw over all leaders and try to figure out which is 3X, which is 4X, and so on. Give up and go buy some new leaders. Buy tippets of various strengths, too, and tell the clerk in detail how you tie on a different kind for every different kind of water. It will impress him, and may impress you enough to inspire you to try it. Try to trick him into showing you how to tie on a tippet without actually asking him, which would cause you to lose face.

Take all flies out of fly boxes in which they have been crushed for months and try to straighten the hackles. Impress your wife by steaming them at the tea-kettle spout. Then go buy some more flies, which you are going to do anyway.

Get the waders out and find the leaks in them. Try to patch them with patented patches, then take them to a filling station and get them patched. Tell the man who patches them that you're not getting new ones because you don't mind freezing water anyway. Later, when you buy the new ones, having said it will be a comfort to you.

Look up all your absolutely essential extra equipment, such as field glasses, flask, rule-scale, cribbage board, hook hone, notebook, camera, floating thermometer, compass, wading staff, first-aid kit, portable radio, pruning shears to free flies from branches, and fish-caller. Dig up some pipes and try again to learn to smoke them, ignoring the way they bite your tongue, dry your mouth, and put a billiard ball in your throat. Fishermen have to smoke pipes.

Then get up on the apartment-house roof and practice fly-casting. The television antennae, radio aerials, clothes lines, and baby carriages will serve as trees, bushes, barbed-wire fences, and other fishermen. If the roof is graveled, so much the better: it will rake the finish off your fly line and give you an excuse to buy another.

Don't wear your fishing clothes and waders on the roof, if you can resist the temptation. People would laugh at you. Wear your business clothes and impress them by being casual. When your line wraps around a TV antenna, pretend you were casting at it. If you happen to pull it down, don't worry; its owner was probably looking at an idiot program anyway.

And don't bother to put all that stuff away carefully tonight. You're going to have to spend a couple of hours collecting it next Saturday morning, anyhow. But be sure to follow the ritual first, or nobody will regard you as a serious trout fisherman.

Fishy Equation
Has No Dry Flies on It

There must be some kind of equation to express the relation between the use of small dry flies and the use of the truth. There are men alive today who have used them both, probably, but not at the same time.

If anybody has any figures on this, he could make a statistician happy. Just picture the digitarian working ecstatically for weeks over that data, with glowing eyes and little shrieks of pure joy, and in the end converting it into something like this:

Let F represent the actual use of Number 22 dry flies and T represent the use of the truth. $F:T = 1:20$. The figures probably would prove out, but everybody would know they lied; the truth is not employed twenty times more than anything connected with fishing or anything else.

People do use Number 22 flies and catch fish with them, and I am sorry to admit it because it is a sad commentary on the human race that men will go to such lengths to catch poor little fish. But it does illustrate the power of the human body to endure pain, because fishing Number 22's is torture. It is like watching a horse race while blindfolded.

Dick Wolters of Ossining, who claims the world chub championship of Susquehanna Road, prepares his own torture by tying his own Number 22 flies. It can thus be said of him that he deliberately uses Number 22's. It is bitter to report that he takes fish with them regularly in the fine waters of Westchester County.

He and his wife Olive took a blindfolded guest to his secret stream Saturday and outscored him in an underhanded way. Wolters, after applying the blindfold, drove for two hours to reach the stream only twelve miles from Ossining.

The water was in summer condition, a little cold, but at an ideal level. There were plenty of brown trout and a few brookies in it, some of them wild fish, but few anglers. Wolters said later that he had fished all day with Number 22's. He has never been convicted of perjury.

It must be said without equivocation that he took five trout and released eleven. He had something like fifty rises. All of his fish were legal, but the best measured about ten inches. Mrs. Wolters went downstream and took a fat thirteen-inch wild brown and wouldn't tell what she took it on. She had not been caught digging worms before the trip began.

Wolters claims that he can see a Number 22 fly on the water and watch its float. He is a man who will rigidly tell the truth sometimes, but nobody credits the incredible, except horseplayers and the Pentagon.

The guest, freed of his blindfold after he was well into the woods away from the road signs, caught a couple of fair trout. He could have caught more if he wanted to, but he was trying to prove that those trout wouldn't take a Number 14 or Number 16 fly, and he proved it.

He was trying, in the pure spirit of inquiry, to discover the truth, knowing that the truth would set him free. It did not set him free from Wolters' claim that he can see a Number 22 fly throughout its float.

A Repertoire of
Copper-Riveted Lies and a
Scraggly Beard to Swear By

A few days around the sleek cabin cruisers and costly gear of the competitive big-game anglers sends the frightened mind staggering back in a search for something more believable. There must have been a time when the strong, hardy outdoorsman fished or hunted with less pomp.

The frightened mind passes quickly over the stale picture of the farm boy fishing with a bent pin and a piece of string. No boy ever fished that way willingly. There has to be a better picture, and there is.

Take the old man who once lived in happy squalor aboard a houseboat in a salt-water inlet. When I was a boy, I thought him the most enviable human in the world and I have found no reason to change my opinion. He didn't have to go to school, or take a bath, or change clothes. He didn't have to go fishing or hunting unless he wanted to, and he could go the minute he wanted to.

This old man said he had been a sea captain, and he proved it often by wearing an old marine officer's cap. The fact that nobody ever called him anything but Cap proved it double.

From the front porch of his houseboat, Cap could catch red snapper, speckled sea trout, croaker, whiting, sand trout and, above all, catfish. In the marshes back of the inlet, he could shoot all the ducks and geese he wanted with his 10-gauge. The woods beyond were full of deer and turkey.

But Cap never caught or shot anything he didn't mean to eat or sell, and he rarely bothered to sell anything. He was a sportsman who had things reduced to essentials—all he ever needed was a few kitchen staples, cut plug, a few shotgun shells, a little simple tackle, and whisky. A few days of guiding or muskrat trapping now and then provided that.

None of the owners of glittering cabin cruisers could even begin to lie in the same class with Cap. They haven't got the time. Cap had lies all ready at any time about the years that he didn't spend at sea on windjammers, alligator hunting, whaling, anything.

He was far ahead of his time. In those days people used to think a lie had to be copper-riveted to make it good. Cap spent hours welding the seams of any lie before he put it on the market. The man would actually have given up lying rather than release a makeshift product. Such a man, living in freedom without credit, has pride.

In addition to all that, he could clinch any lie in a way that no big-game competitive angler can clinch one today: he swore by his own beard, a scraggly gray tangle that compelled belief.

And that is the focus of the whole thing. Nobody can believe the boats, tackle, and accoutrements used by the big-game anglers of today. Or the distances they travel, super first-class, to get to their fishing, or even the monstrous fish they catch. It can't be so.

But anybody can believe a six-pound channel cat caught off a houseboat porch with a cuttyhunk line and a slaughter pole—and fried in lard. With that solid basis, and a good beard to swear on, any man could calmly relate, and be sure of full credit, that he strangled a sixteen-foot alligator by ramming his arm down the alligator's throat.

We ought to get back to reality.

Unsuccessful Goose Hunters
Cultivate Southern
Drawls as Consolation

Belhaven, North Carolina—This River Forest Manor is a place where hunters from north of the Potomac temporarily lose their grammar and gain a temporary Southern accent, of sorts.

They do this largely by associating with Southerners who go to Maine and return home talking like Down East guides.

A Columbus (Ohio) businessman, who was graduated from Northwestern University a few years ago, after three days' residence here was heard to say quite seriously to his guide:

"I ain't had nary a shot at a goose today."

He went on to state gravely that he solid wanted to get him a couple of geese and shore would feel some kind of shamed to go home without he toted some feathers with him.

The guide, Harold Williams, looked at him curiously; but, being by nature courteous if not mild, he said nothing. He never had heard any gabble like that before, even from a Yankee, and couldn't figure out a reply that would satisfy both the man and the possibility that the man suddenly had taken leave of his senses.

I also heard a distinguished medical man from Philadelphia say to Axson Smith, the operator of this place, which now seems to be the last stronghold of the Confederacy:

"Ax'n, I'm fixing to git my gear together for tomorrow. You reckon we got a chance for some nice misable weather?"

Smith replied absently that he thought it quite possible that the morning would bring rain and wind. Then he did as startled a double-take as any ever seen on the stage. It is difficult to understand why he was startled; that sort of thing happens a dozen times a day here.

Smith himself contributes to this general confusion, not so

much because of a Southern accent, which he has by honest right, as by a certain freedom of fancy when discussing hunting. Smith passed up goose hunting today for ducks, and came back in the afternoon with a vague story that he had killed "about" seven.

This was accepted, or at least not directly disputed, although nobody, except perhaps the kitchen help, had seen any ducks. But Smith cannot let a good thing rest. By 6 P.M., he had reached the point of asserting that he had killed one of these ducks by looking at its reflection in the water and firing a mirror shot.

He said he didn't make a practice of that kind of shot but had done it just to show that he could. By seven o'clock, he was saying that his mirror shot was at ninety yards and at a right angle.

"It ain't rightly to my credit," he said modestly, consciously reverting to type and causing two New Yorkers and one member of the Ohio Old Order Amish to make mental notes for later use. "It's just a gift my daddy learned to me."

This is shameless promoting. Smith, who absent-mindedly lapses into grammar when he is not watching himself, knows that, if a hunter goes home gooseless and deerless, he will be satisfied for a few days with a phony Southern accent.

Those who have killed geese, and most of them have this week, only will spread it on a little thicker until they finally interpret correctly a certain look in the eyes of their wives.

See you-all later.

Butcher's Secret Battenkill Badger Is Trout Anglers' Ultimate Weapon

Shushan, New York—Secrets are what Okey Butcher deals in. He trotted out three of them today for an evening of trout fishing in the Battenkill, without revealing their inner nature. Butcher's secrets have a singular quality: you can see them, but you can't understand them.

He began today with his secret bug repellent, which he makes from either sweet fern or pennyroyal; he is a little vague about that, maybe because he has not yet untangled the secret himself. It is a liquid that doesn't hurt fly lines. Bugs don't seem to bite with it any more than they do without it.

Butcher's fly dope, which is austerely named Butcher's Fly Dope, is a more important secret than Butcher's Bug Repellent, which is a new concoction and will not have the sanction of antiquity for several weeks.

It is a liquid, too, brewed in secrecy in the same Shushan barn in which Butcher mixes all kinds of secret trapping and hunting scents and mails them to about twenty thousand customers. He doesn't care to say what is in Butcher's Fly Dope but is glad to drop your fly into his bottle of it.

It works, too. I used several small flies this evening, sometimes in fairly fast water, and Butcher's Fly Dope made them ride about as cockily as anybody could want. Butcher doesn't list his fly dope for sale, though it could be that a fisherman might buy some of it if he played his cards right. Butcher is a sucker for a sob story, accompanied by a buck or two.

Butcher unveiled his third secret after we had stepped into the Battenkill and fished awhile. Trout were rising everywhere in a flat run and shallow ripples, but we could not identify what they were rising for. I tried several smallish flies and caught a brown trout on each, but none of them brought the kind of ready action that the rises had indicated.

It was then that Butcher, timing his big moment with the instinct of the born showman, unveiled Butcher's Secret Battenkill Badger, a dry fly that is not a copy of any living thing. It has badger hackle and tail, no wings, and a body that might be anything.

The singularity of this fly lies in the fact that it is guaranteed to kill on the Battenkill but nowhere else on earth. Elsewhere it is merely a superlative fly.

Butcher is willing to identify the secret of Butcher's Secret Battenkill Badger, but it won't do anybody any good because only Butcher can tie it. He says the secret is that even a fairly good fly-tier can't tie so sloppy a fly and a good fly-tier can't even come close.

The secret, therefore, lies in human nature. Ordinary mortals who tie flies cannot help but do their best. Irresistible urges, rooted in thousands of years of human striving for beauty and searching for natural truth, sweep them helplessly on in a sweating, grunting climb toward perfection.

But not Butcher, the man who deduced without effort that brine would lure porcupines to the trap and proceeded logically to sell brine. He is a man who can do his worst any time he wants to. Since he knows that the worst is often the best, it never inspires in him the inward struggles of the immature mind.

He says Butcher's Secret Battenkill Badger was the worst he could do, and with practice he has got so he can do it every time. And it would be hard to question that it is the best. He tied one on for me and I caught four nice browns in the few minutes before it got lost in a willow tree. It wasn't my fault: I didn't plant the tree there. Besides, my foot slipped.

Butcher didn't care. He can tie a dozen flies that badly in a few minutes with his eyes open. As that there man said, nobody else can do it even if they are dead.

The limit on the Battenkill is five fish. We each took three and released maybe eight or ten. Butcher took the biggest, fifteen inches. Wouldn't say what he took it on, so he must be building up another secret.

Behold a Hunter (and His Tent and His Beeswax, His Wife and Children)

Jimmy Salvato said over the telephone that a great many people in New Jersey had stopped worrying about fishing and were immersed in preparations for long hunting trips to places such as Wyoming and Alaska. He said truly that such activity kept a man tied up for weeks.

This doesn't bother Salvato very much, since he operates the Paterson, New Jersey, Rod and Gun Store and is not especially reluctant to help outfit hunters. He is an old bear killer himself anyway.

But it bothered a hunter who lives in Ossining and is now preparing to be rugged this year, and it is now bothering his wife and two children. Everybody in the house is under his whip, working like slaves to get Daddy fitted for sleeping out.

This man thought he had to have a tent, so he went and bought one. It cost twenty dollars and was guaranteed to sleep two adults, both dry. It was made of light nylon, and the salesman muttered something about thirty-three threads to the woofle and twenty-eight to the zagreb. It had tent poles that folded up so small that they could be lost in a watch pocket, and four corner tie-downs with nylon ropes.

Well, this hunter, whom we will call Galileo for short because he hath an inquiring mind, took it home and tried to put it up in the living room. He couldn't do it, but his twelve-year-old son and four-year-old daughter figured it out in the end and set it up.

They moved it to the yard, and Galileo put the children in it and turned the hose on it to see if they would get wet. They got wet.

Galileo went out and bought some heavy nylon to make an

envelope to put over his tent. He and his wife cut the nylon, and she stitched it on the sewing machine while he guided it through. They put the sheath over the tent, stuck the children in it, and got them wet again with the hose.

Galileo heard somewhere that melted beeswax would waterproof a tent, so he bought some. His idea was to melt it, paint the nylon tent floor with it, and then test it. For some time he couldn't figure out how to get the children under the tent floor for testing purposes without smothering them. He did it in the end, however, by propping it up on the sides. This time they didn't get wet, but they insisted on another hosing inside the tent but above the floor, and they were running out of dry clothes.

The tent had weighed three pounds, so the salesman said, when he bought it. Now Galileo was afraid to weigh it and was making plans to hire a trailer. And he hadn't yet beeswaxed the outside of the tent. He now had nineteen tie-downs instead of four. The tent has cost him roughly a hundred dollars.

On weekend fishing trips he was spending all of his time planning tent improvements, and, when he and the family returned exhausted, he kept them up far past midnight stitching, beeswaxing, and putting the tent up and taking it down. Nylon rope stretched too much and he bought cotton rope, which stretched too little, or vice versa. His living room was a sweatshop.

I haven't heard the last of this yet, and I am afraid to tell Jimmy Salvato about it. Salvato says people enjoy making preparations for camping trips. He is a gentle, sensitive fellow, and I don't want to destroy his faith. But how much can a wife and two children take?

Pheasant Hunters, Despite Unquestioned Abstemiousness, Found Prone to Gout

Hunters have enough troubles, even discounting domestic explosions over hunting expenses, without Dr. Robert E. Van Demark of Sioux Falls, South Dakota, who has stepped forward with some more bad news. He says pheasant hunters are prone to acute gout.

There is something inappropriate about this. Gout has been the subject of jokes for centuries, but pheasant hunters are deadly serious men who speak humorlessly and endlessly of the frosty mornings and the glories of autumn. There is no levity in them.

Also, gout is irrevocably associated in the public mind with wealth, and no respectable pheasant hunter will admit that he can afford to buy the equipment he needs; some of them can scarcely scrape up the funds for an eight-hundred-dollar shotgun. In Old England, gout was always linked with torrents of port, a costly beverage, but it is well known that pheasant hunters seldom get very drunk.

But Dr. Van Demark, all the same, speaks with authority. He speaks in the South Dakota *Journal of Medicine and Pharmacy,* and South Dakota is a state that entertained 128,119 hunters from every state in the Union in 1956.

The proneness of pheasant hunters to gout does not lie altogether in the pheasant, although its rich meat does contain an uncommon amount of purine bodies, something or other that helps to cause gout.

No, there are other and unkinder things to say. "Additional causes are: trauma of the feet in walking through fields and gullies, the overindulgence in holiday alcoholic beverages, the fatigue of excessive exercises in those unaccustomed to it, and gorging on delicious and well-cooked pheasant and high-calorie foods at the end of the day."

Not a pleasant picture of the pheasant hunter—a drunken, gluttonous, lazy fellow with traumatic feet. Van Demark might have been more charitable or, as the word runs relentlessly now in literary circles, compassionate.

He then goes on with professional pleasure to describe the intense pain of gout; the swollen, tense, stiff, blue great-toe joint; the dilated nerve, and other matters that doctors like.

Something can be done about it, of course: rest, elevation of the foot, hot packs, opiates, analgesics, a cradle to protect the foot and draw the attention of jokesters. And with systematic treatment, Van Demark concludes happily, "Prompt recovery is the rule."

The pheasant hunter is then ready to go pheasant hunting again and renew the cycle—unrepentant, unchastened, and eager for rich food, rich liquors, and unaccustomed exercise.

Well, the pheasant hunter's life is full of pitfalls anyway, and a little gout will not make his burden unsupportable. What hurts will be the pitiless jokes—all of them dating from before the American Revolution—and the big toe.

Safety and Fashion Note: Shotguns With Colored Stocks Get the Business

There must be some kind of fascination in selling stuff. Harrington & Richardson, makers of good shotguns, has just announced that it will sell shotguns with brightly colored stocks.

This is a serious matter, you understand, not just a way of selling more shotguns. Harrington & Richardson thunders the names of the United States Army, the National Rifle Association, and the Optometrists Association in the opening broadside of its announcement.

123

These three great organizations have conducted tests that prove yellow is the color most easily seen and recognized; therefore, for the sake of safety, H & R will make some of its shotgun stocks yellow.

There will be other colors, for other reasons, but the company, based in Worcester, Massachusetts, pins its faith in safety firmly to yellow. The company darkly cites the National Safety Council, another resounding name, for authority that twenty-two hundred hunters met with accidents last year. Reading between the lines, it is plain that the figure could have been diminished considerably if everybody had carried a yellow-stocked shotgun.

There are hunters alive today, and I am one of them, who prefer to be not too visible to other hunters in the field, on the theory that if the other hunter cannot see you he cannot shoot you. Or that if he cannot see you clearly he may miss you.

This view is anchored to hundreds of newspaper stories of hunters shot by other hunters. In most of these cases both parties are dressed from head to foot in scarlet, a color that is easily recognizable and seldom worn by deer, pheasants, bear, or rabbits. Yet H & R clings to the faith that the hunter most easily seen is least likely to be shot.

"We feel the use of colored gun stocks is a major forward stride in the development of hunter safety," says William G. Krebs, national sales director of the company.

In further pursuit of safety and other things that Krebs pursues, stocks will be produced in red, blue, green, purple, pink, and black. Those pink and purple stocks ought to make hunting safer than hard money.

But the company modestly introduces another note here. The selection of tasteful colors, the announcement says, will offer women an irresistible opportunity to make their shotguns part of their field ensemble. Thus, a lady of the field, having chosen pink bird pants for a day of quail hunting could lift from the rack a shotgun adorned with a baby-blue stock.

But ugly complications could enter at this point. Suppose her station wagon was green? Or she had no baby-blue hunting boots? Or, even worse, she might be hunting with an Irish setter of coarse red. Imagine the turmoil if her male companion of the

124

day showed up wearing green pants and carrying a red gun stock, the peasant boor! There would be no choice; she'd have to stay home.

This sort of thing is dangerous, tampering with the most sacred articles of our faith that clothes make the man and woman. It may be safer, but is it good taste? What will the International Association of Dress and Hunting Clothes Designers, Cosmeticians, and Dermatologists say?

Such explosive subjects are better left alone.

Point Judith Survey
# Indicates You Can't Take
Tuna Fishermen Lightly

Point Judith, Rhode Island—An exhaustive analysis of the United States Atlantic Tuna Tournament, which ended here yesterday, plucks a clear conclusion from a miasma of doubt:

Tuna anglers, as a class, are fatter than surf-casters.

There can be no doubt about the validity of this conclusion, which may come to be known as the Point Judith Axiom. It is hardly possible that so many ponderous men have been gathered in any one place for any purpose except maybe to wrestle.

The anglers in this tournament must have averaged a good one hundred and ninety pounds. Many of them, who stood nineteen hands high or more, are bound to have gone to two hundred forty pounds.

Trained investigators were set to work on the question and they have come up with some interesting stuff. The problem, of course, was to find out why tuna anglers are bigger than surf-casters. Depth interviews among several thousand bystanders who came out daily to view the dead fish brought out these documented facts:

1. Tuna anglers have to be more prosperous than surf anglers

125

because they must own or charter costly boats. A surf angler needs only a rod, which he always refers to affectionately as an idiot stick, a reel, and a few odds and ends. Therefore, tuna anglers eat better and drink more milk shakes.

2. Tuna anglers sit all day in a fighting chair, not fighting fish except once in a while. They just don't get any exercise.

3. Men proud of their strength turn naturally to tuna fishing, though bull strength is not necessary. Mrs. Eugenie Marron of Brielle, New Jersey, who stands five feet tall and cannot reasonably be expected to win the next Olympic weight-lifting championship, catches giant tuna, black marlin, and other monsters. Still, tuna fishermen are mostly big, strong men, and proud of it.

4. Tuna anglers don't have to be agile, but surf-casters of the true old fiend breed do. Boss Bill Backus of the Elizabeth, New Jersey, *Journal,* chief judge of this tournament, is the prototype. He judges all day, writes a story in the early afternoon, and casts in the surf for stripers all night.

Backus can catch tuna if he wants to, but he doesn't want to. He wants to catch striped bass in the surf. He is a lean, leathery type, designed especially to climb around on slippery rocks in the nighttime, which he does. Tuna anglers only have to be agile enough to swivel a fighting chair.

5. It might be argued that surf-casters are more energetic and therefore less inclined to adiposity, yet tuna anglers are not lazy men. They get up at about 5 A.M. and often have been seen after midnight ashore, holding on to furniture from habit.

There may be other reasons, but the shoreside spectators, who are expert on everything about fishing, didn't know of them. The Point Judith Axiom is firmly established, but more research is needed on the deep, underlying causes. It would be a good project for a foundation.

As Any Fisherman's Wife Can Tell You, Catching Salmon Is Child's Play

Ludlow, New Brunswick—The Miramichi is up about a foot after yesterday's rain and the salmon fishermen here can't do anything much. One of them did bring in a grilse this morning, another played a salmon for five minutes and lost him, and a third got a short rise.

The deal is, according to the wise old heads, that the river will drop a little tonight and tomorrow things will improve somewhat. It is a good story, anyway.

This is the kind of day for the woman who was here last week with her husband. The fishing was good then and she couldn't understand why he didn't bring in a salmon for two days. What was so difficult about it?

The husband explained carefully that salmon didn't strike every fly that came along, but she was not convinced. What was the use of coming up here if he wasn't going to catch salmon?

On the third day he caught a ten-pound salmon and his wife met him at the landing of Eldred Bailey's Camps. She was very pleased with the fish, but why only one? Next day he sent her out with a guide after explaining that the thing on the end of the leader was a fly and that it should be cast upon the water.

About two hundred feet from camp, just upstream from a highway bridge, she hooked a twelve-pound salmon on her first ten-foot cast, though the fish had to pick the fly from a tangle of line and leader. She hauled it in briskly and was back at camp with it inside of twenty minutes. What was so difficult about that? she wanted to know. Why couldn't he get a salmon every twenty minutes? She was very suspicious about the whole business.

Bailey asked her how much of a run the fish had made. She

didn't know or care. How could she tell? Well, did the fish run out all of the casting line and get into the backing?

"What's backing?" she inquired curiously. "Is it necessary for fishermen to use such curious language? It seems to me that they do that just to make a ridiculously easy thing look hard. I can't see anything complicated about salmon fishing."

Her husband, according to Bailey, was a man of iron self-control, one who had schooled himself, in years of marriage to that lady, to flinch at nothing. Bailey said she left here alive.

In the same week, Bailey got a telephone call from a woman in New York whose husband, a doctor, was fishing here. The doctor was asleep, at 9 P.M., and she seemed mildly surprised at that but didn't want to awaken him. How was he getting along?

"Pretty good," Bailey was able to reply. "He had a fish on today, but lost him."

"He did!" she squealed in astonishment. "Whereabouts?"

There are some women at this camp with their husbands now, but they have heard these stories and are trying to figure out what they mean. Meanwhile, all three of them are very guarded in their conversation about fishing. None wants to raise the first unaccountable laugh.

There is little laughter among the men, except the polite kind when clean jokes are told. Salmon fishermen can find little to laugh about when the water is high. But a drop tonight might bring a giggle or two.

Why Johnny Can't Read
Between Lines of a
Barefaced Tale—Or Can He?

It seems that modern education isn't giving enough basic information about hunting and the woods to the children. Of course, they can get a course in how to make a penwiper out of a squirrel tail, but that isn't basic.

Only yesterday a friend named Witherspoon was trying to explain to a ten-year-old boy how Witherspoon had supported his family in Louisiana when he was ten years old by catching wild bears alive and selling them to zoos. The boy's gaps in background knowledge were so wide that Witherspoon had a hard time making him understand.

Witherspoon said he had been wont to ride his tame trained bear to school. The boy wanted to know where he got the bear, and Witherspoon explained that he got it like anybody else got a tame bear: he inherited it.

He went on to relate that after school every day he rode his bear into the woods. The boy wanted to know then whether he had a saddle, and Witherspoon patiently explained that bears thought it silly to wear saddles and you had to ride them bearback.

129

He continued that, when they found a wild bear track, his tame bear would put his nose to the trail and take off, crossing rivers and bayous full of floating ice and scrambling up and down mountains. The insatiable kid wanted to know then how Louisiana got ice and mountains. But you can't train a boy in meteorology and geology in five minutes, so Witherspoon had to let that go.

He said, when they caught up with the wild bear, he would jump off his tame bear and start teasing the wild bear with a switch. The quarry would chase him up a tree, he said, and he would crawl out on a weak limb, with the bear following, until the limb broke.

Then, he explained, when the wild bear hit the ground, it would be knocked cold by the impact. He said he would then————. But the kid demanded to know why Witherspoon was not killed by the fall. Patiently, Witherspoon explained that that was what a trained bear was for. It had caught him. The kid had never thought of that.

Well, said Witherspoon, he would then tie the wild bear's front legs together and his hind legs together, and shove a strong pole between them. He would lift the back end of the pole and he would get on the tame bear and ride home.

The confounded kid demanded to be told which was the front end of a pole and, anyway, how could the tame bear hold up one end of it while Witherspoon————

But never mind. You can't explain anything to a kid as ignorant as that. He just didn't have the background knowledge that he should have been given in school or somewhere.

Witherspoon was trying to give him some useful information that might enable him to earn some side money when he grew up to wear charcoal gray. But the boy couldn't grasp it. No basic education. All he did was ask progressive-school-type questions.

Tricky, Those Wildlife
Agents, but Our Man
Has Broken Their Code

Many a little gem of information and piquant prose winks and flashes in the *Fish and Wildlife Report* of the United States Fish and Wildlife Service.

This periodical public document bears at its top the dignified name of the United States Department of the Interior, Fred A. Seaton, Secretary. But it is unlikely that Seaton wrote all of it and he might not have written any of it.

Is Seaton, a former Senator who was once in the newspaper business, capable of inventing the waterfowl-day-per-acre? No, no, his training in these occupations, rigorous as it might have been, could never have prepared him for that. Only a biologist or a statistician could soar to such depths.

This jewel was added to the statistical diadem, adorned already by the passenger-mile and the fisherman-day, in a report on waterfowl in the Back Bay-Currituck Sound area of Virginia and North Carolina.

The report begins with the thundering statement that thirteen aerial surveys made last fall, winter, and spring had revealed that "waterfowl spent an estimated 12,613,000 waterfowl-days" there.

This, the report noted with quiet pride, was "an average of eighty-six waterfowl-days-per-acre."

To what use can these two facts be put? Are they merely hanging statistics? Of course not. Any amateur statistician, slobbering with joy, can divide that 12,613,000 by that 86 and come out with the acreage of the Back Bay-Currituck Sound area used in the waterfowl study—146,663! That is a thing worth knowing, and there is a lot more satisfaction learning it that way than in just being told.

131

In another little study, the report says water skiing on most wildlife refuges is bad for wildlife. But it doesn't say the thing in just that way; biologists and people like that have to be dignified and a little mysterious. The report says water skiing is being permitted in areas where "such recreation will not react adversely to wildlife."

Now that "react adversely" in itself is special language, and pretty ripe stuff, too. But what is doing the reacting here? Why, "such recreation," which means water skiing. And it is reacting adversely to wildlife. So we come up with the brand-new maxim that wildlife ruins water skiing. If Seaton had written it, the sentence might not have come out that way, but then he is only an ex-Senator.

There is some more fine adverse reaction in the report on the use of antibiotics in coyote control, which means killing coyotes. The problem here is that poisoned meat, set out to kill coyotes in hot parts of the West, spoils too quickly.

A couple of government agencies with long names began fooling around with antibiotics and came up with one that would keep the meat relatively fresh. And it would do this "without adversely affecting feeding by coyotes."

This is really pretty subtle stuff. Apparently it means that, although the meat is relatively fresh, the coyote will eat it. This seems to imply that coyotes don't like fresh meat but that poisoned fresh meat kills quicker and cleaner than poisoned spoiled meat. But wouldn't that in itself result in "adversely affecting feeding"?

One gets the impression along here somehow that the government really wants to adversely affect the coyote but doesn't want to say so. Seaton could have learned that in the Senate, but still it doesn't sound like Seaton talking.

Hunter Shoots a Gobbler
and Spends Rest of
Day Crowing About It

Camilla, Georgia—It is a brutal act to shoot one of a man's wild gobblers within a few feet of him while he is strolling along without a gun, convinced that the turkey hunting is over for the day.

But that is what Charley Dickey did to C. B. Cox this morning after an hour or more of shivering on the banks of the Flint River. Dickey, apparently oblivious to the cruelty of the thing, showed no regret later. Cox took it in good part and by late afternoon seemed to have forgotten the matter except for an occasional scream of agony.

Yet the man was cut to the quick. Cox and his partner, Woodrow Brooks, operate the Riverview Shooting Preserve here. And Cox sees to it that his guests shoot plenty of quail and a few chukar partridges. But he does not promote turkey shooting; he and Brooks reserve that for what they call their private entertainment.

It was double fault for Dickey to do a thing like that. As southeastern representative of the Sportsmen's Service Bureau, it is his pleasure and duty to promote shooting preserves and to help their operators, not to kill their turkeys.

Dickey took me to the banks of the Flint just before dawn today while Cox was taking Jack Seville of *Sports Afield* magazine on a little turkey walk east of us. Cox and Seville covered three or four miles, walking awhile and yelping awhile with Cox's slate-and-cedar turkey-call.

Dickey and I sat with our backs to opposite sides of the same stump while Dickey tried to call turkeys. Nothing happened for an hour, and it was a raw, windy hour. Nothing happened for another half hour.

133

Cox and Seville meanwhile returned to Cox's pick-up truck and drove it to within two hundred yards of us along a woods road. The horn wouldn't work, and they walked, without guns, toward us to pick us up. Cox stopped to sound his call.

At that moment turkeys began to call from three directions on our side of the river and from across the river. Seville jumped a turkey in the woods road and, empty-handed, watched it fly away. He and Cox jumped another on the steep river bank and almost could have hit it with a stick.

A gobbler called about two hundred yards north of us, and two or three minutes later a hundred yards southeast of us. No more than a couple of minutes after that, it was clucking fifteen yards away in heavy brush. Dickey was facing it, and I didn't dare turn my head to look. Wild turkeys spot any movement instantly and take off.

The gobbler's head rose above the bush, and Dickey shot him dead. It was a magnificent shot, fully fifteen yards, and it was worth noting that Dickey was using high-brass Number 6 shells in his 12-gauge shotgun. Yet he didn't brag much about the shot later—not all of the time, anyway.

It didn't seem necessary for him to mention more than half a dozen times that Cox was supposed to be a master turkey hunter, yet had not shot a turkey. It hardly appeared essential for him to laugh coarsely when Cox claimed to have called the gobbler up for him.

It was clearly not vital for Dickey to ask Mrs. Cox eight or ten times whether her husband had ever brought home a turkey. He might have avoided questioning Brooks about whether his partner knew there were turkeys on the place.

But, on the whole, he was pretty gentlemanly. He offered to let Cox have the tail-fan to hang in his lodge, provided he printed Dickey's name under it in suitably large black type.

Self-Confessed Stellar
Turkey-Caller Winds
Up by Getting the Bird

Camilla, Georgia—It is possible to report tonight that Charley Dickey's fires have been damped if not quenched, and that the man at last can be readmitted to the society of humans and turkey hunters.

This happy situation came about through no special virtue of Dickey's, though he is widely regarded in some places, sometimes, as a man of dazzling virtues. It developed through the inexorable forces of nature. That means that wild turkeys have got his number.

Some days ago Dickey called up and shot a gobbler. It changed his character, and not necessarily for the better. Within five minutes after the shot, he had pledged his sacred honor to call one up for me to shoot.

An hour later he was kindly instructing C. B. Cox, who operates the Riverview Shooting Preserve with Woodrow Brooks, in the art of turkey calling. Cox was glad to get this instruction; he has been hunting turkeys around here for only thirty years and hasn't got them figured out yet.

It got so that a man couldn't sleep at night here for dreaming of Charley Dickey's turkey and of Dickey's gobbling, yelping, clucking, and gabbling. Dickey began roughing out the outline of a book on turkey hunting in North America and queried the New York office of the Sportsmen's Service Bureau, of which he is the southeastern representative, on whether he could copyright a certain low hen yelp he had worked out.

But Dickey made a mistake, one of the few of his lifetime. He took me out next morning, and next afternoon, and the following morning, and the following afternoon. He placed me artfully in brush cover and set out to yelp up a turkey for me.

135

The rest of it is brutally simple. Dickey didn't yelp up a turkey or get an answering yelp. During the middle of the day he began to miss quail shots that formerly he would have considered set-ups. Cox was extremely generous and forbearing about the whole matter, never riding Dickey about either the turkey calling or the quail shooting for more than forty minutes of any hour. Yet Dickey began to get a hang-dog look.

His wife Evelyn stood loyally by him, showing no sign of shame at any time. When she muttered something about how she might have married a thirty-covey plantation owner, everyone was pretty sure she meant that she was glad she hadn't.

Dickey took me out again today, and again late this afternoon, to yelp up a covey, but the story was the same. He is worrying now about his sacred word of honor, for Dickey is said to be an honorable man.

It is a sad thing to see a fiery nature subdued, a great spirit broken. Yet it may be best for society. Dickey might have become an incendiary social force.

He is back now to his Sportsmen's Service Bureau duty of advising and helping Cox and other preserve operators in the management of game and guests. This afternoon he downed four quail in a row, including a spectacular cross-shot, and got one double.

The bureau is hereby advised that it will not be necessary to destroy him.

Deer Prove Elusive
in Maine Woods, but a
Hunter Can Learn a Lot

Vienna, Maine—Beer has more calories than whisky, the deer-hunting woman said in the beech woods today, and therefore she confined herself virtuously to whisky, though not while hunting. She said that that took character, which it does, and that it was a beautiful day, which it was, and that the deer weren't moving about to any astonishing extent, which they weren't.

This woman was hanging around on a fine old logging road running through the hardwood along the edge of old spruce choppings, and she was not secretive about what she knew and had seen.

She hadn't seen much today, but she knew a heap, especially about deer. The deer were not messing around much in the beeches and oaks, she said with ringing authority. This was so: I had been rattling around in those hardwoods from early morning until late afternoon and had seen only one fresh pawing. So had Lee Wulff of Shushan, New York, who owns the woods we were in. And his wife Kay had been sitting silently in those woods all day without hearing or seeing any deer.

The woman said with equal authority that the deer were skulking in the swamp, and for all I know they were. They may also be skulking in the thick spruce and pine and birch and ground juniper on the knolls along the swamp edges. I don't know about that, either. A short pass through that stuff, wet, noisy, and exasperating, was enough for me.

Wulff made considerable of a traipse through it, though, and he didn't jump anything that he knew about, or see any fresh sign.

This woman was full of solid knowledge. She said it didn't

do no harm to smoke on a deer stand, for example. The smoke was going to go downwind, she said, and a deer would get your scent downwind anyway. She said it even figured to help a little, since a deer might smell the smoke and move toward it out of curiosity.

She said the only reason she didn't smoke on the stand was because she didn't smoke at all, but she was figuring on taking it up pretty soon because it cut down on the appetite for sweets, which were full of calories. Not that she was fat, she said; everybody told her she had kept her figure pretty good. But it could slip up on you.

The woman had plenty of sound medical knowledge. Deer hunting was good for you, she ruled, because it exercised muscles that didn't get exercised any other way.

She wasn't exercising any muscles at the time. In fact, she sat so still that I walked within ten feet of her without seeing her. She informed me that that was the way to get deer. It is, too.

She saw Wulff come through, too, and he didn't see her, though he was farther away than I had been. Wulff was doggedly trying to see something or hear something and had been trying for about nine hours. A little later, on the edge of an alder swale, he heard two sharp blats from a deer. But it was dusk by then, and he didn't see anything.

Just the same it was the score for the day, except for that valuable information about calories.

Does a Bear Have Fleas?
Your Guess Is as
Good as Goldilocks'

Shushan, New York—An old public debate, simmering on the back burner for years, has been revived here, and feeling is running high.

The issue is whether bears have fleas.

One group of bitter partisans holds that since bears are furry land animals, they must have fleas. They are the deductive-reasoning crowd. Their enemies, exponents of scientific observation, reply that these people have no clinical proof.

The question was raised years ago in a letter to O. L. (Okey) Butcher, who sells trappers' supplies by mail and is the inventor and purveyor of many animal scents, including buck lure and lures for racoon, mink, otter, fisher, badger, muskrat, and other furred beasts.

Butcher, who has trapped all his life and was a pioneer in the use of scents instead of bait, is widely supposed, among the twenty thousand persons who receive his highly personalized catalogue, to know everything. The scents he cooks up in his barn are held to be proof of it. People ask him questions by mail. They often run like this:

"How many traps do I need? I am twelve years old."

A fourteen-year-old, with two more years of intellectual beef, asked him many years ago whether bears had fleas.

Butcher, who had skinned many a bear, either never had noticed or could not remember. But he answers all queries, and this reply was masterly. He said that some bears did.

But this boy was not to be put off by the language of diplomacy. He wrote back that he wanted no more beating around the Butcher: he wanted to know whether *all* bears had fleas.

Butcher pondered for a week and came up with another

139

brilliant manifesto. He said that he had not seen all bears and could not answer for the ones that had evaded him, being a man who would never bear false witness against bears. But, he said, he knew that *some* bears had fleas and beyond that a scientist could not go. He judged that would hold the little meddler.

He was never wronger in his life. The obdurate kid wrote again, and severely this time, demanding a clear answer. He wrote still again, relating that he had asked a question-and-answer editor in a magazine and that this walking encyclopedia had replied didactically that bears did have fleas.

But the editor had been overcome by an attack of acute cowardice and had added that, since bears had fur, they might reasonably be supposed to have fleas and, therefore, as a general sort of a thing, he would assume that they had.

This insufferable kid could not be put in his place. He scouted around until he found a hunter with a fresh-killed bear, and found fleas on it. He triumphantly wrote this news to Butcher.

But Butcher is a man who can be dangerous when aroused by an ignorant child. He replied with stiff dignity that the boy had proved nothing by finding fleas on one bear. It was necessary, he pointed out with scientific rigor, not only to examine thousand of bears, but also to have a control group living under the most antiseptic conditions.

No child can buck that sort of thing; it is adult stuff. The boy gave up as far as bear fleas were concerned, though he has since, in the pride of his manhood, bought more than five hundred dollars' worth of trappers' supplies from Butcher.

But the dispute had got out of hand. Old hunters and trappers in this region had got wind of it and had taken sides in the uncompromising way of outdoorsmen. Brother was arrayed against brother. The civil war raged for years before it finally subsided to occasional guerrilla action and then died out.

It is going again now, started by a visitor's ignorant remark, and it may be years before the roar of forensic fury subsides. But this country is still safe for visitors. These people don't let strangers into their feuds.

Despite Tradition,
Hunters and Anglers Have
Right to Shave in Woods

A young man shaken by anxiety walked into Jim Deren's
Angler's Cove in the Chrysler Building a couple of days ago
and wanted to be told authoritatively whether a fisherman or
hunter was bound to refrain from shaving while fishing or
hunting. He said he wished to respect tradition but hated not
to shave, for whiskers made his face itch.

Deren, sensing that he was being put in the switches, tried to
evade the issue by selling the young man a fly box, but the
young man was too worried to concentrate, and the sale was
lost. But Deren wouldn't be committed.

There was no need for Deren to take that attitude. The question can be answered with clarity and vigor.

A man of character will shave in the woods if he wants to.

It is true that iron tradition demands that a man who spends
a week in the woods must emerge with a week's beard. It is
true that all outdoor magazine covers prove that all strong,

hardy outdoorsmen always have at least three days' growth when shooting a deer or catching a trout.

It cannot be doubted that women consider facial stubble manly, virile, and physically attractive. All good Western movies are based solidly on this principle. I do know women who make the irrelevant claim that gray or white whiskers are not necessarily irresistible, but it is to be noted that the claim is always made in reference to their own husbands. Many a man has won a woman by appearing before her fresh from the primeval wilderness, atavistically bearded and dirty.

Nor can it be doubted that a few days of not shaving rests the face and adds tone to the hide. It also camouflages the frighteningly sallow face of man, making him less startingly visible to the trembling deer or vigilant crow.

Most of all, nonshaving hunting or fishing gives civilized man his last chance to see how he looks in a beard—how he might have looked in another and more masculine age. There is no other way to achieve this end, except mountain climbing, which has no other purpose.

Yet Deren was wrong to dodge: he should have reiterated the rights of freeborn Americans, ignoring the sneers of the slavish who lack courage to shave in the face of public opinion.

The plain fact is that a man of character will shave in the woods or in a hunting camp if he wants to. If he is a man of moral courage, he will do it in plain sight of whiskered companions watching in silent contempt, and stare them down. It may take added valor to go back to town and appear barefaced before women who know he has been in the woods, but a man of principle will do it, and Deren ought to have said so.

I know a man in Vermont who shaves every day in the woods, and he is respected just the same. Unfortunately, I cannot use his name. There are libel laws.

If 100 Men in 516 Hours
on 9 Streams Catch 220
Fish...How's That Again?

The recent discovery of the angler-acre-day opened dazzling avenues of fishing statistics, but its discoverers purblindly failed to see them. It is incomprehensible, as if a man watched a desert sunset and saw nothing but desert.

An Eastern state's conservation department discovered the angler-acre-day, which expressed how many anglers missed how many days of fishing on how many lake acres because something happened to the fishing there. The state regarded this as a dead and tragic loss, apparently on the theory that anglers who would have fished this water didn't fish anywhere.

But that is not the point; the state missed the point entirely. It was not missed by the New World Society for the Exploration of New Fishing Statistics (est. 1961). Since I happen to be the society's Actuary-in-Chief, I am in a position to outline something of what the society has seen merely by looking into the sun.

In the first place, this day business is sloppy and unprofessional. Fishing days differ in length. The hour is the correct unit—and it provides bigger statistics, which is the aim of all statistical reckoning.

And the acre is no good, either. It ignores trout streams, because a stream cannot be measured credibly by the acre. The mile is the correct unit. Therefore, the Angler-Hour Mile is your true measurement of fishing lost or gained or just realized.

Let us suppose, for example, that 100 anglers in one day fish 516 hours on 122 miles of nine streams and catch 220 trout. Eliminate the 100 immediately: there are 516 Angler-Hours. Multiply by 122 and you get 62,952 Angler-Hour-Miles or AHM.

Now 220 fish is an average of 2.2 fish per angler. Thus the average AHMF or Angler-Hour-Mile-Fish would be 13,739.4. But the absolute AHMF would be 13,739,440, and we are getting into pretty respectable stuff, right up there with the airline passenger-mile.

Again, AHM (62,952) equals 220F, a very nice equation, which can be advanced to 62,952 over 220 equals 1F, and this works out to 1F equals 286.14 AHM.

We are now already far beyond the angler-day-acre child's play, and without any real investigation yet. That will come later, after my retirement as Actuary-in-Chief, an office that I accepted only reluctantly and temporarily.

It is enough to point out that by applying the same sound mathematical principle, Miles (M) can be expressed by an equation with AHF, Anglers (A) can be limned as MHF, and Hours (H) as AMF.

And we haven't even brought up those nine different streams. Something like 8.214 other statistics, the society's I.B.M. machines reckon, can be adduced by multiplying and dividing these above figures, one at a time, collectively, and at random.

It is inexcusable stupidity that these things should have been overlooked. The brilliant future of fishing statistics is at stake and we are at a crossroads. If nothing is done soon to exploit these potentialities, I am going to take it up with the Bureau of Labor Statistics. Fishing is hard work.

"Packet" Is Fine for Fishing in Cold Rain; an Old-Fashioned Fire Helps, Too

Greenville, Maine—This day was a sort of study in transportation as it concerned fishing and bad weather. The results, as collated here tonight, were numb feet, sore muscles, exasperation, ten blueback trout, and a big fat brookie. An analysis of results can wait until the Russians make their next move.

Everything hinged on the weather, which was windy and overcast this morning, as it had been for two previous days. But the cloud cover was high enough for Lee Wulff of Shushan, New York, to get his float plane off Lake Minnehonk at Mount Vernon, Maine, and fly it to Wadleigh Pond, some fifty miles north of Greenville.

That was all right for Wulff, sitting in the pilot's seat. But I shared the rest of the two-seater with something its manufacturer calls a Packet. A Packet is a round, collapsible canvas boat with aluminum ribs. It is made on an ancient, even prehistoric, design: that of the coracle, or what the Irish call a currach (or curragh).

The Packet carries in its folds an aluminum chair, which can be fixed into the boat when it is extended, and a pair of aluminum cars. The works, fitted into the rear of a two-seater plane, does nothing for the comfort of the passenger, or deadhead.

It does nothing, especially, when the plane is bumping through curtains of rain and gusts of wind over mountains that do not look soft. Wulff seemed to be unconcerned, but then a pilot is bound to seem unconcerned, or what is the use of being a pilot?

He got the Supercub into little Wadleigh Pond, set in a cup in the hills about five miles west of Lake Allagash, without any trouble, and there was no difficulty in tying it to logs. But it was cold and raining up there, and by the time that was done and the Packet was set up, my hands and feet were numb.

It was then that I resorted to an old pioneer's trick to get warm in the woods: I built a fire. Modern man, enslaved by the marvels of modern technology and bemused by insulated boots and underwear, hand-warmers, parkas, and trick jackets, has largely forgotten this ancient stratagem of the woods. Too bad; a fire in the woods is better than a third straight natural with everything riding.

Wulff tried the Packet first, since it was his and he deserved the risk. The thing figured to be a cork in the wind, and, since it was round and had no keel, it should have spun around unmanageably. It did turn with the wind, but those aluminum oars could spin it back just as quickly.

Wulff had no trouble. He managed to catch four blueback trout, which are said to grow only in Wadleigh, and a fat brookie weighing about two pounds. Meanwhile, I waded the shore till I was numb again. Then I resorted to another old frontiersman's gambit: I built another fire.

It was then my turn to use the Packet, and it seemed to me at the time that I stepped into it with faultless aplomb—on the outside. The fact that water along the shore was only three or four feet deep has nothing to do with the matter; it takes iron self-control to maintain faultless aplomb in a round canvas boat in rain and wind. Wulff agreed to that; he said a man was bound to have a stiff upper lip if his face was frozen.

It was not difficult to manage the canvas boat, wind or not. It did have a tendency to spin in gusts and currents, but correction was easy. Handling a six-and-a-half-foot fly rod in it was easy. I took a couple of bluebacks on a muddler and returned to the plane. It was no time to change outdoor tactics: I built a third fire.

Meanwhile, Wulff had picked up three or four more bluebacks by casting streamers from the shallow water. We packed the Packet in the airplane, Wulff packed me in with it, and we flew through the rain to the Holt Flying Service dock here. Wulff didn't have any trouble getting out of the plane. He and Roger Holt didn't have much trouble getting me out of it.

A Fisherman Must Be Honest
With His Wife, but
Sometimes It's Difficult

This is the kind of thing that a fisherman should never do, because honesty is the best policy, though if it is a policy it is not honesty. The point is that an angler ought to deal plainly and fairly with his wife—in some things.

This man had just bought a seventy-five-dollar bamboo rod when I entered the tackle store. It was being put into a shiny aluminum case.

"Be sure to get all price tags off it," he said to the store operator. The operator giggled: good joke.

"No, no!" the buyer said in alarm. "I mean it. This is serious."

"Oh, sure. A gift, huh?" The salesman was trying to catch up. But he was still far behind.

"No, not a gift," the man said patiently. "This is for *me*. I wouldn't buy nobody a rod like this. I'm thinking about my wife. What I'll do, I'll go home and tell her I picked up this piece of damaged junk for five bucks. She won't know the difference and she'll think I got a hell of a bargain. Women go for bargains.

"You leave that seventy-five-dollar price tag on there and she'll rip and tear for about an hour and then sulk for three weeks."

Now it has to be admitted that the man is smart and that he is considerate. He loves his wife and he is willing to make any sacrifice to save her from the torture that women have to endure when men spend seventy-five dollars for fly rods that could just as well be spent on new drapes.

But is he honest? Can love long feed on tricks and guile? Where are the limits on connubial trust? It is a knotty ethical problem, but clearly the fisherman is wrong. What should he do?

Well, he can't go home and callously announce that he has spent seventy-five dollars of her dough on a fly rod. That would be brutal, as well as very dangerous. Love won't long survive on defiance, either. Ultimatums and harsh announcements of the *fait accompli,* or money spent without permission, threaten the very fundaments of our domestic institutions and are pretty likely to make our American women violent.

He could sneak the rod into the house while she is mixing the evening milk shake and hide it where she would never find it: in her bedroom clothes closet. That would be clever, kind, and considerate because the rod would never come to her notice. But one of the children, rummaging for hidden Christmas presents, might haul it into the light and blow the whole gaff. Unsafe.

He could buy a cheaper rod, for sixty dollars maybe. But that would dissatisfy him and satisfy nobody else. He could hide the rod at a friend's house, but you can't trust anybody with a fly rod.

The thing seems insoluble, but it is not. There is a sound, honest, fair, loving, considerate way to handle it, if a man sets his mind to it, and if the wife is a nonfishing wife.

All he has to do is get the rod gift-wrapped, take it home with a fatuous smile, and present it to her as an advance wedding-anniversary present. She couldn't wound his loving heart with petulant objections then, could she? Especially if he could get the tackle store operator to give him a fifteen-dollar receipt and the florist to make up something pretty nice.

Honesty is what counts in these matters. Our American domestic institutions are based on it, and an American fisherman ought to be able to get a rod without being treated as a treacherous outcast for three weeks.

Seven-Year-Old Girl Baits Her
Father and He Flounders
on Her Fish Lines

Here comes Harry Forgeron of Baldwin, Long Island, deliberately pitting himself in a writing contest against his seven-year-old daughter and never suspecting that he and all other adults are outclassed. It is pathetic.

There is nothing left to do but lay it out chronologically and let Forgeron, the sucker, take his lumps. First came this letter from Chatham, Massachusetts, direct, clear, austere, elegant, and graceful:

> Dear Mr. Randolph,
>
> I went fishing today on Cape Cod. I caught two butterfish. I am seven in a half years old. My father is 38 years old. He didn't catch any thing.
>
> Sign, LAURA FORGERON

The scene now shifts to Baldwin. The Forgerons are home, and Forgeron is fretting because his own daughter has put him in the dozens by writing to a newspaper. Now is the time Forgeron makes his sorry error in judgment, his decision to answer. But I will hand this to him: he doesn't write anything about how sharper than a serpent's tooth it is.

He did try to save what dignity he could, and it was a brave effort:

> Randolph:
> Regarding my daughter's letter:
>
> It is not true that I am upset about this butterfish incident. It is also not true that I was upset when she skunked me at flounder fishing on the Cape in June.

149

And I'm only mildly concerned about this kid's technique, in which she foul-hooks fish with a flounder jig. What she doesn't hook in the mouth she catches by the tail.

But now I am on the receiving end of remarks such as, "Cheer up, Daddy, maybe you'll be lucky next time." One of these days—Pow!

HARRY FORGERON

He doesn't know when he is well off or what his chief hope is. His chief hope is that this girl will grow up and forget how to write such prose. That she will do. She might forget how to fish, too.

Maine Defends Rustic Life. Won't Let Hunter Fined There "Charge It"

Maine may have made a costly mistake a month or so ago. A visiting hunter was collared for a game-law violation and tried to pay his fine with a credit card. The judge made him get up the cash.

Earle Doucette reported this matter, and mark that he did it for the State of Maine's Department of Economic Development in a press release. In other words, Maine didn't even suspect that it was doing anything wrong. It was ingenuously telling the world, when it might have kept quiet.

What's going on up there, anyway? Doesn't the state want any business? Everybody knows that people lose face nowadays when they pay cash; it's vulgar, except in Maine. The state is never going to get anywhere with its fall hunting business until hunters are able to open accounts in various courts of the regions they aim to hunt, and sign for their fines, with tip added for warden.

Let's face it: these are the times when hunters wear socks wired for heat; these are the times when more men hunt from automobile than afoot; these are the times when a man needs seven specialty guns in order to hunt at all. Why should the courts of Maine remain mulishly out of the great American credit facility?

This is distressing to me, because I like the State of Maine and I like Earle Doucette, who naïvely revealed the court's mean insistence on cash. A state just can't keep up with the hunting trends without a very limber judicial credit policy in the day of hot socks and duck-blind bridge games.

The Department of Economic Development will find that neither Maine nor any other state can attract the complete, modern, hot-socks hunter until it is made possible for him to walk into court and say easily: "Put it on my cuff, your Honor."

At the other end of the East Coast, Florida ought to be establishing easy court credit, possibly even with a layaway plan. It is incongruous, in fact way out of proportion, for a man who hunts quail from a complicated palmetto buggy worth five thousand dollars and carrying six expensive bird dogs to be compelled to dig for a measly fifty dollars in a grubby courtroom.

And what about those hunting lodges where the strong, hardy outdoorsman pays around a hundred dollars a day for bed and board and quail hunting, with Jeeps or mule wagons to haul him elegantly from covey to planted covey? Such hunters just don't carry cash; it makes their pockets bulge.

It is true that they don't get arrested much either. Still, such an outdoorsman might feel better and like a state better if he knew he could stroll into court and take care of his rap by a gentlemanly lift of an eyebrow or a friendly nod to the judge.

The state might even work out a judicial credit card of its own, not only for hunters but also for all other delinquents. There is sound reason to believe that collections of fines for hunting offenses might make a great leap forward. This is a source of public revenue that has hardly been touched and certainly has not been developed.

It is ridiculous that a man who can buy his car, his guns, his hunting equipment, and his gas on credit, stay at a hunting

151

lodge on credit, and buy his wife a present to square himself on credit, can't violate the game laws on credit. The judge could always add a nominal carrying charge.

I'm working on another angle now, but am not ready to make an announcement. If this works out, a hunter will be able to cuff his jail sentence with the right card. The Diners' Club, American Express, and the Hilton Hotels haven't had time to answer my queries yet, but they probably won't see any serious difficulties.

There is no limit to the future of hunting if it is financed in the modern way.

Fly-Tiers Are Urged to
Keep Abreast of Times
and Pick Names Accordingly

Something like 8,416 wet and dry flies are being invented today by 6,314 of the 168,829 men and women who are satisfying their winter fly-tying craze while auditing the sincere inanities of television jollyboys. The other fly-tiers, contentedly free of the lonely hunger of creativity, are tying standard patterns.

These are the figures gathered by the statistical division of the American Society of Digit Lovers and endorsed by fourteen distinguished clergymen, none of whom can explain why so many clergymen like to tie flies.

Most of these 8,416 new flies will be named, though it is the height of chi-chi among trout fishermen to carry to the streams austerely unnamed inventions of their own. It doesn't matter whether these things catch fish: any angler can lie a little, though 99 per cent of them are sorry hands at it.

But it is time that somebody protested against the fly-naming policies of those who do name flies. Fly-naming has fallen into disrepute largely because nothing new has been introduced in this century.

It is all very well to name flies after famous fishermen—Gordons, Hendricksons, Wulffs, etc. But there aren't enough famous fishermen to go around. It is also sound practice to give some of them descriptive names, such as Blue Dun Spider. Or to combine the two policies in one name, such as Jim Deren's Harlequin because Jim Deren invented it and it has gold ribs in diamond shapes. But there is no real dash in descriptive names.

It is time that fly-tiers got abreast of the times and named their creations for events of public importance. This is the Age of the Tie-in, and fly-tiers especially ought to realize it.

There is nothing new in naming flies that way—it is old and tried. Nobody will be able to top the brilliant naming of that Rogan of Ballyshannon who was an ancestor of Alex Rogan, the great contemporary fly-tier. He named one of his The Coming of the Orange Parson to Baleek in ironical celebration of the arrival of a clergyman sent to Baleek by William of Orange. It is still catching salmon.

But the name can be imitated and the fine old policy reinstated. A few names were suggested last night at a meeting of Gough's Indoor Outdoor Forum in Forty-third Street. None of the forum members has ever tied a fly, but any member will name anything any time. And they are all keenly interested in important public affairs.

Buddy Coen, for example, got the floor (by outroaring Martin Gough) to advance a brilliant name:

The Dodgers are Still Bums.

Matt O'Brien, a sleepless student of world news, endorsed Coen's proposal and offered a sound one of his own:

The Eddie Fisher Loves Elizabeth Taylor.

John Dugan, a man deeply read in diplomatic affairs, was pleased with O'Brien's motion, but thought a profounder note ought to be introduced also. He composed:

The Sparse Gray Dulles Flies Again.

There was some prim objection to that one, since forum members are men of sober moderation, sometimes, but all

153

hands unanimously adopted the important name sponsored in a fiery speech by Sam Kan, and the meeting was adjourned without fighting. Kan tied his composition expertly to current history of an importance that cannot be exaggerated:

The Edward R. Murrow Interviews Zsa Zsa Gabor.

Well, there are a few sound suggestions. Any fly-tier should be able to take it from there, and break away from the tired, unimaginative old names. We have got to have fresh, vital stuff that is new, new, new.

Our Man Gets Wind of
Plan on Coast to Ban
Cheese as Bait for Trout

New York fishermen are hereby warned that there is an insidious movement afoot in California that may well spread insidiously eastward like the aroma of old Liederkranz and strike insidiously at the very foundation of their inalienable rights.

In brief, an official of rank wants to ban cheese as trout bait. This is the kind of thing that could eat away the beams of freedom.

Carl Wente, a fish and game commissioner in California, is

the figure looming darkly behind this major assault on liberties. Jack Curnow, the outdoor columnist of the Los Angeles *Times,* is the champion of public rights who blew the whistle on him.

Curnow says in his column that Wente has tried this thing twice before and been defeated both times, "which you'd think would be enough to convince him that the public likes to fish with cheese."

With all due respect to Curnow's public spirit, it seems to me that he misses the point. What difference does it make whether the public wants to fish with cheese? Or whether an angler will fight another angler over the relative allures of fine old imported Gorgonzola and Vermont sage?

The question is whether it is constitutional to forbid a man to fish with the cheese of his choice even if he doesn't want to. Our forefathers did not fight a bitter war of liberation in order that the wholesome products of the honest dairy should be forever barred from the pellucid waters of our rivers and rills.

New Yorkers are not famous as cheese-anglers. There are men alive in this city right now who have never caught a fat rainbow on an artful lure of Bel Paese, or even a hunk of marbled Roquefort. But every freeman here was born with the ineradicable right to the free, unhampered, unabridged use of delicatessen.

Curnow says that, as near as he can make out, Wente just thinks cheese is unsporting and that Wente has no other coherent argument. The hole in this thesis is readily apparent to any sportsman. If cheese is unsporting, so is milk, and if milk is unsporting, so are babies. Where would family life in America be if such a position could be maintained?

Curnow says Wente is a fishing purist, and he thinks that is all right. But, he asks, why should Wente want to shove artificial bait down the public throat when the public hungers for healthful cheese? There is no satisfactory answer.

The Fish and Game Commission will hold a meeting this month at which, Curnow says Wente has announced, Wente will try again for the noncheese rule. Curnow issues a ringing call to sportsmen to fire wires to the commission opposing this sumptuary regulation.

It will be well for New York anglers to remember that this

is a dairy state, and that dairy owners often own fishing waters, and that it would be an ill thing for the state if they rose in fury. George Washington had to send out the troops to quell the Whisky Rebellion. Let us have no Cheese Rebellion here.

America's Cup Contest
Finds Our Man All at Sea
Concerning Yachting Talk

Newport, Rhode Island—This was a fine fishing day off Block Island, and several hundred boats of all sizes were moping along the America's Cup race course, but nobody in sight was fishing. That was where democracy went wrong; it was a mistake adopted by unanimous vote.

Yet the public is never entirely wrong. Several thousand people were learning to talk sailage, a tongue with a number of English cognates. And for about a cigarette-while, they seemed to be seeing a boat race.

Even in that brief moment, when *Columbia* and *Sceptre* (it is sleazily vulgar to use an article before the name of a sailboat) were crossing the starting line, it was no Kentucky Derby. Watching this race was about like watching a game of mental chess.

Watching it from Ralph Evinrude's yacht *Chanticleer* was the way to watch a yacht race, if there is any way to watch a yacht race. The *Chanticleer* is a hundred-and-eighteen-foot, up-stairs-and-downstairs cruiser with a veranda on top and about twenty-six pairs of strong binoculars lying around on deck furniture.

It seems as if Evinrude, who makes outboard motors, ought to hate sailboats. He ought to spend most of his working hours knocking them. But such is not the case. He mentions them kindly and speaks sailage fluently, though with an American accent. He knows, for example, that the mainsheet is a line, which is a rope.

Several guests aboard, who had Long Island accents, were equally fluent. It was child's play, therefore, to learn that *Columbia* and *Sceptre* crossed the starting line about even, but that *Columbia* was upwind, which was termed good.

These people made it plain with many a nimble idiom a few minutes later that *Columbia* was pointing into the wind better than *Sceptre,* and this was deemed to be something pretty special. Both boats seemed to be standing still, but sailage made all clear.

When *Columbia* rounded the first mark, spread her spinnaker, and made off on the crosswind leg five minutes ahead of *Sceptre,* no alien tongue was required to explain the situation. Sign language, such as shrugs, was enough from that moment until *Columbia* crossed the finish line about a mile in the lead.

Yet there was fascinating talk of Genoas, jibs, coming about, falling off, and stuff like that. A couple of trips like this, and a strong, hardy dryland-type outdoorsman could speak pretty fair sailage, with the help of a little pidgin English and eloquent hands.

There were other advantages, such as time and comfort to talk about fresh-water fishing. A man who said his name was Red Smith and who talked broken sailage indicated in another language that he could whip anybody who denied that the State of Wisconsin's bass fishing was as good as any other state's.

Nobody denied it, and he went back to the rear of the boat to ask Evinrude who was ahead. Evinrude said *Columbia,* and Smith said yes, *Columbia* certainly could point into the wind good and had therefore been able to grab the pole. I think he meant by this that *Columbia* was a better boxer.

This Fourteen-Year-Old Can Hunt,
All Right, but Will He
Learn to Talk Hunting?

Westkill, New York—Jim Stafford, Jr., came back to Art Flick's
Westkill Tavern Club after a day of woodcock hunting without
any special or evident desire to give his father a hard time.

But, without boasting, he was willing to state the facts. And
the facts were that Jim, Jr., fourteen years old and therefore
just old enough to hunt with a licensed adult, had killed two
woodcocks while his father had killed only one. This was the
younger Stafford's first hunt, but not the first for his father.

Furthermore, under merciless cross-examination, Jim Stafford, Sr., who lives in Smithtown, Long Island, with his family,
admitted that the son rated an assist even on the father's bird.
In fact, Senior conceded on the stand that he could not swear
that his shot and not Junior's had downed that bird.

This situation is not uncommon, and it is the best sort of
training for a smart boy: it gives him material with which to
learn how to talk hunting. Nothing is more important.

Jim, Jr., for example, can make great play with this material
around school in Smithtown, and the sooner he learns how to
do it properly the better. Any mention of this hunt around school
must be made in such a way as to force questioning; the entire
story must not be dumped out baldly. The appearance of a
modest reticence must be rigidly maintained while the boy com-
pels his listeners to elicit the story in detail.

Thus it is all right for him to admit reluctantly and casually
that he killed two woodcocks, but he must never add that his
father killed only one. Not voluntarily. He need only remark that
Jim Stafford, Sr., an expert hunter and gun hunter, was there
to teach him hunting and hunting safety, and that the law re-

quired a fourteen-year-old boy to hunt only with a licensed adult.

Any listener who does not then inquire how many birds the father killed is too much of a dolt to be worth talking to at all and can be dismissed contemptuously. Girls may not have sense enough to ask it immediately, but they can easily be led into asking. And, if necessary, a male straight man can be enlisted to ask the question in the presence of girls.

The boy in this situation must be shrewd enough to understand that his father should always be represented as a fine shot and a crafty hunter, if for only one reason: it is better to outshoot a fine shot than a poor one, and a son who hunts with a good, experienced hunter will be assumed to be a knowledgeable young hunter. This impression can be built up by casual references to shotgun gauges and actions and shot sizes.

Such material is great stuff with girls: they do not understand it, are not interested, and cannot be impressed with it. Yet it gives a boy a masculine, worldly air that may stagger girls a little, maybe. A casual modesty helps here, too, because girls love quiet, modest boys almost as well as they love loud, confident boys. But hunting material should not be overused with girls, who grow cranky if they hear too much of it, unless the boy is exceptionally good at dancing the cha-cha-cha or may soon get a sports car.

In the home, a boy should be extremely cautious about the use of any material to the effect that he outshot his father. His father will tell it first, with pride, and the boy would do better never to repeat it or make too much of it.

Ordinarily, he may depend on some other member of his family to keep it alive, and even then it is good policy to deprecate his own triumph and make sound excuses for his elder. Fathers can stand just so much.

On the whole, a boy who kills more game than his father the first time out has the finest kind of outdoor talk material—if he uses it with art and restraint. By leading and nudging conversations delicately, he can make it last for years—or give his father that impression anyway.

Fish Leave Brodhead Creek
and Remove Kink
From Angler's Personality

Henryville, Pennsylvania—Ernest Schwiebert got called George Schwiebert by somebody or other a couple of years ago when Ernest's book, *Matching the Hatch,* came out, and the error put a kink in his character. The kink almost was straightened out today by a brown trout in Brodhead Creek.

Schwiebert advised me this morning to start with a Hendrickson fly. I started with one of Lee Wulff's new plastic-bodied flies and caught a foot-long brown on the first cast. But Schwiebert crossed me up by taking a bigger one on his first cast with a Hendrickson.

His character kink straightened out to some extent right then. I could have called him George again and put him back in trouble, but a spirit of generosity overcame the urge to exercise power. Anyway, he had caught three or four more browns on that Hendrickson before I thought of it, and then the situation was past mending.

Richard Wolters of Ossining was at the same time taking three or four pretty good browns—he said later that he was, anyway. Jim Rikhoff of New York, also reported taking a few. The odd thing about it was that both said they had released all of their fish. This probably was the truth. I have seen them keep fish, but still, maybe they did release some.

John Falk of White Plains wasn't doing much, and admitted it. Alvin Ziegler, who operates Henryville Lodge and owns the water we were fishing, couldn't understand this. He pointed out kindly to Falk that the Brodhead was full of fish, which it was, and that everybody else was either scoring or saying he had scored.

This is private water to the extent that Ziegler owns it; but it is public water to the extent that anybody can fish it for a daily fee of five dollars. Ziegler stocks it, and there are some native fish in it, too.

It was no trouble to take fish this morning on dry flies. I caught brown trout—all of them eleven to thirteen inches—or got strikes on five standard patterns. Falk finally got a good fish. Schwiebert took and released a dozen. Wolters said he caught fish.

After lunch, Schwiebert, his character only slightly kinked by now, thought it time to live up to *Matching the Hatch*. He got out a wooden box full of feathers, silk, and stuff, and clamped a fly-tying vise to it. He tied some hatch-matching flies, including a little caddis pupa, grinding his teeth savagely while he tied.

It turned out that he did live up to that book about what fly to use where and when. He caught thirteen good brown trout in one pool with the caddis pupa, and managed not to be objectionably modest about it.

At about that time, a big brown was breaking my leader for me. He had come up to a Henryville Special, a dry fly sold by Ziegler, and missed it twice. Then he seized a kattermann, another Brodhead favorite, and that ended our business together. In fact, it finished me for the day.

Schwiebert, now kinkless and singing, kept right on taking browns, with pupae of several kinds, little streamers, dries, and anything he wanted to throw. The hatch couldn't have been that various, as I pointed out to him kindly, but he took the position that he had matched it, anyway.

Hunter or Angler Who
Can't Lie Well Will Be
Happier if He Lies Low

There isn't much doing in the fishing line hereabouts right now, and hunting won't start until tomorrow, so this is the time that hunters and anglers give full exercise to their gift of knowing everything about everything in their line.

It is not a unique gift: all high-school seniors have it temporarily, and all editors have it permanently. But the manly outdoorsman uses it incessantly and therefore develops it to a higher and more complex degree.

The complexity is subtle. For example, there is no virtue in pretending to know a specific, provable thing, even though the outdoorsman really doesn't know it. He understands nothing of ballistics, but he can listen wisely to a discussion of a certain rifle load, throw in a vague but knowing remark, and come off as a pretty knowledgeable fellow. But it is a thing anybody could look up in five minutes, and there is no honor in pretending to know it.

When he goes to buy his deer-hunting ammunition, he will walk into a gun shop and say: "Gimme a box of thirty-ought sixes." If the clerk asks him whether he wants 150-grain or 190-grain, he has only to reply:

"Well, hm, it's kind of brushy where I'm going but not too brushy. Let's see, now . . ."

All he has to do then is stall until he finds out what the salesman thinks he ought to have, ratify it as if it were his own choice anyway, buy it, and walk out with the purposeful air of a man who knows what he wants and has got it.

But it is no triumph; anybody can do it. An outdoorsman grows in his own eyes only when he can pretend to a deep and detailed knowledge of fish and game that can come only with long experience and keen observation.

For example, he is exchanging polite lies in some milk bar with other trout fishermen as ignorant as he. Water in all the streams is so clear, low, and warm that nobody has caught anything lately, though, of course, nobody says so. The discussion therefore turns to crafty ways of getting strikes in those conditions.

This is a set-up for a fast man. It seems that only last week, by an exercise of great ingenuity, he had caught a big one in low, clear, warm water. He was fishing the Beaverkill, and he found a good ledge just below the mouth of a cold brook.

He knew there had to be a brown trout under that ledge, but he also knew it wouldn't take a fly presented in the customary ways. He sat down on a rock and figured it out.

Instead of casting his stone-fly nymph a little upstream and letting it slide by the ledge, he got directly opposite the upstream end of the ledge, cast it directly across, let it sink, and then let the current take it at an angle away from where he knew the trout was, instead of parallel to the ledge. A flash of color! Whang! Twenty minutes of artful play. Seven pounds, twelve ounces.

He hasn't found any such ledge. He hasn't caught a brown trout in a month. He hasn't been to the Beaverkill in two months. But he has fashioned a good round lie that argues he is a man who knows trout and can think for himself.

These are about the only good lies fishermen and hunters ever tell. They are not even to be associated with the childish exaggeration-lie—about the fish that lowers the stream three inches every time it jumps, or twaddle of that sort.

Hunters lie a bit better than anglers, probably because they have more scope, but even they lie best when there is a purpose to the lie—the purpose of portraying themselves as knowing just about everything there is to know in the woods.

Any hunter worth knowing who missed a standing deer at forty yards last November ought to have the event dressed up by now to a great piece of reasoning on where the deer would be, a crafty stalk, and a difficult downhill kill through brush on a dark day. If he can't put himself away as a combination of

163

Natty Bumppo Uncas and Daniel Boone, he ought to stay out of milk bars.

It is irrelevant and immaterial that he may be the greatest bore in Christendom. He's smart.

Ice Anglers Would Rather
Be Caught Dead Than
Caught Contemplating

If there were any truth in the proposition that fishing is the contemplative sport, it would be ice fishing that would attract the heavy thinkers.

Of course, there is no truth at all in that soggy old piece of corn pone. People stop thinking when they start fishing and merely experience sensations such as heat, cold, wetness, sunburn, fatigue, and the stimulating bite of the black fly.

But an ice fisherman could think if he wanted to. It is easy for him to get himself into a state of suspended, or frozen, animation resembling the trance of a Hindu mystic. Gazing steadily by the hour at an unmoving tip-up is bound to bring about self-hypnosis. If the fisherman were not a fisherman, the mind would be free to soar.

But there is the rub: the guy is a fisherman and would therefore rather be caught dead than contemplating. His mind is not fascinated by reflections on his relation to the universe but by drowsy pondering on the liveliness of his minnow. It may turn now and then to admiration of his hardihood in enduring discomfort, or to wondering whether he will ever be able to feel his feet again, but it will never lose itself in speculations on the nature of truth.

The ice fishermen, who are busy now with their chilblains on Lake Champlain, are blood kinsmen to the surf-casters, some of whom are still doggedly hurling bait at stray Long Island stripers. They are men who have to prove, and do frequently prove, that they are superior to the elements and to pain.

But while the surf-caster is a man who loves solitude and hates the sight of his fellow man while fishing, the ice fisherman is as gregarious as a honeybee. It is a pleasure for him to know that his neighbor's feet are also frozen, and to compare sensations with him. The sight of little huts, tepees, and windbreaks huddled together on the bleak ice gladdens his heart.

Well, these fellows are at it in the far North now, vigorously cutting holes in the steel-hard ice, working hard to keep them open, sniffing the invigorating north wind with stiff noses or waiting with stoic patience for the tip-up to tip up.

It is a fine sight to see, and distance lends it enchantment.

Trout fishermen, on the whole, don't care for it. Why would a man want to fish in the dead of winter when he can wait until the middle of April and fish in running water? On snowshoes probably, and with frozen fingers, or in a freezing rain, but still in running water.

Better to spend those winter months standing knee-deep in wet snow or shacking through thick laurel on a steep New England mountain, hunting snowshoe rabbits. A strong, hardy outdoorsman has got to have some sense of proportion, and to a trout fisherman and rabbit hunter, it is plain that these ice fishermen haven't got it. A man must curb his love of discomfort somewhere.

Fishing and Hunting Stories
Collected by Jurist
Are Strictly Legitimate

Montgomery, Alabama—As an angler, hunter, and farmer, J. Ed Livingston collects fishing and hunting stories as other men collect game trophies or hotel ash trays. As Chief Justice of Alabama's Supreme Court, he collects legal fishing and hunting stories.

Some of the informal stories sound pretty near like the truth, and, of course, nobody would suspect the Chief Justice of Alabama of stretching one of them, very much.

Livingston's legal fishing and hunting stories are naturally nailed down by opinions and rulings of record. He says he can cite the records, and it would be contemptuous to doubt him. The fact that he is an angler and hunter who is neither silent nor secretive is irrelevant, immaterial, and incompetent. He is a Chief Justice.

His favorite citation quotes Judge Ben C. Dawkins, Jr., in United States District Court, W/D Louisiana, Shreveport Div., Crim. A. No. 14098, in United States of America v. Alvin Dowden, as recorded in 139 Federal Supplement, Page 783. Nobody can doubt and none but lawyers can understand that.

Dawkins freed Dowden of a charge of killing a young buck deer whose horns were not three inches long. The case came into the Federal Court because the deer was killed in Kisatchi National Forest. Federal law says deer killed on Federal reservations must conform to state requirements, and Louisiana requires hunters to kill only bucks with horns three inches or more long.

Judge Dawkins, deciding without a jury, flourished a jocund pen in his decision, which began:

"A tiny tempest in a tinier teapot has brought forth here all the ponderous powers of the Federal Government, mounted on a Clydesdale in hot pursuit of a private citizen who shot a full-grown deer in a National Forest."

The judge, having so imprisoned his tempest and caused it to give birth to Federal powers on horseback, proceeds to ridicule the Government's charge that the deer was a fawn. The evidence showed, he said, that it was an adult buck, sixteen to eighteen months old, and only unfortunate in having nubbin horns.

He laughed briskly at the Government's "pointing to the lack of points to prove its point" and derided a case "requiring the services of five game agents, two biologists, the opposing attorneys, the United States Marshal and three Deputies, the Clerk, Court Reporter, and a Federal Judge who is a little tired of such matters."

Dawkins then proceeded to try the buck on charges of being a fawn and found him not guilty. One of his five principal rulings in favor of the deer:

"Biologically, he was a buck, not a fawn, who in strictly female company would have had to bow to no critic. His handicap actually was one only upon having to fight for the affections of the distaff side. What he lacked in weapons, he could have made up for in celerity, dexterity, or finesse."

Therefore:

"It necessarily follows that if Buck is not guilty, neither is Alvin, who is acquitted and discharged *sine die*."

Best Way to Get
Fishing Tackle Ready: Admire
a Sucker Who Knows It All

It is just about time for the solemn trout fisherman to start the long spring ceremony of getting his tackle in shape for the coming season. There are several sound and detailed systems for doing this, but by far the best is to play helpless.

Anybody can do this who has suckered a neighbor or a friend into showing him how to put up storm windows. It is the same system, basically that enables a po' little old ignorant Southern girl to get everything she wants, including a Ph.D., from everybody within her orbit.

The thing to do is to admire people who know how to condition tackle, and like to do it. Admire them out loud in their presence, and ask their advice and instruction. Put them in the position of teachers and mentors, men with special knowledge and impossible skills, and yourself in the pose of an ignorant, clumsy but trusting pupil. This creates in them a feeling of irrevocable obligation.

The next step is to get such a man to your own home and show him your tackle and ask just how to proceed. Have the tools and the materials ready, and make a clumsy pass at taking a reel apart. Look at it blankly. Ask him what to do next.

That is all you have to do; he will do the rest. He will replace worn line-guides on your rod, rewind wrapping, sandpaper and varnish the rod, clean and lubricate the reel, examine and dress the line, and even tie up a few leaders for you.

There are other systems, of course, but they are more wearing. They make no sense anyway: if you are a man who can do anything with tools, you don't need a system; if you are not, you will make a mess of it, anyway.

Still, you can try if you are in love with self-sufficiency. Anybody can take a reel apart, probably, in anything from five minutes to two hours, and lots of people can put it back together. Anybody can wash the insides of it with kerosene or dry-cleaning fluid and maybe not set himself on fire. Anybody can wash the parts in water and put too much grease on the gears and too much oil on the points of friction.

And anybody can take the reel to a tackle shop afterward and get the reel repaired.

It is quite likely that 40 per cent or more of the fishermen who own fly rods are capable of determining whether a guide is loose, and some of them can rewind it. A good many persons, most of them fifteen-year-old boys or girls, can sandpaper or steel-wool the varnish from a rod, swab it with lighter fluid to remove oil, and wipe varnish on the rod with thumb and forefinger. They will do it too slowly, so that the varnish will get sticky, and spread it too thickly, and fail to get under the guides with a little brush.

But it will be done, and a tackle shop can always undo it and do it again.

None of this is necessary when the helpless system is used. The helpless system is infallible if a skilled sucker is selected and handled properly. No po' little old ignorant rod-owning Southern girl ever has varnished her own fly rod or been without a fly rod in perfect condition.

Outdoorsman Can Be
Thankful for Wife if She
Allows Him to Go Hunting

This is the day for a hunter to think up something for which to give thanks, and it won't be hard to do.

He can, for example, be thankful that he is alive and un-maimed, if he is. And that he hasn't shot somebody else, if he hasn't.

While he is on the subject of health, he might be grateful for the wonders of modern medicine, since hunters are, on the whole, the greatest pill-consumers the world ever saw. Sorry indeed is the strong, hardy outdoorsman who does not carry ready-made medicines in every pocket. In this habit, hunters are excelled only by farmers.

On the other hand, the thankful hunter may exult because he thinks he is strong and hardy. Makes him feel like the tireless conquerors of a wild continent, while he sits in his insulated underwear and weatherproof parka in a heated duck blind.

Let us all be grateful that there still is some purchase in money, so that we can have three or four more guns than we need, and boots for every occasion, and hand-warmers, and game-calls guaranteed to call game, and pheasants stocked by a beneficent state or paid for by us by the head on game preserves, and five-thousand-dollar automobiles slung low enough to protect a pup tent from the wind, and commercial hunting lodges where we may camp out with hot showers and central heating.

It is a good time for the hunter to be thankful for manners developed by centuries of polite living, which compel his friends and business colleagues to listen while he describes in brilliant detail how he did not kill a deer. It is true that these same manners command that he listen while a golfer tiresomely relates his banal experiences on the fifteenth hole. But if everything were perfect, there would be nothing to be thankful for, except everything.

That will remind the hunter to be thankful that there are still men alive who can lie with skill and restraint, and that he may hope to meet one of them some day, if he lives long enough and searches steadily in the least likely places. And this may make him thankful that he himself has sometimes choked back a silly hunting lie, if he ever has.

Let him also be thankful that hunters bear a strong resemblance to other people and that therefore the great majority of them do not hog shots, cut off game, claim every kill, deliberately invade each other's deer stands, or shoot at anything that moves or makes a noise.

The International Association of Amateur Protocol Directors estimates that the hunters who do these things are in about the same ratio as people who crash parties or hog taxis. Otherwise, everybody would be dead or involuntarily committed.

His best shot, though, is to be thankful that in spite of expense and restrictions and posting and game scarcity and a few other nuisances, he can still go hunting whenever he wants to, if his wife will let him.

All True Outdoorsmen Are
Likely to Sit Inside by
the Fire on Christmas

All true outdoorsmen will prepare today to have the only truly essential thing for Christmas morning: an open fire to bring the outdoors indoors. Nothing reminds man and his family of nature so much as eyes swollen and stinging from wood smoke.

It doesn't matter that the hunter or fisherman will be presented tomorrow morning with shells of the wrong gauge from his daughter, woolen baby socks from his son, and a hunting jacket designed for a television jollyboy from his wife. He has been buying himself Christmas presents for the rough, hardy life afield all year anyway.

That fire will square him away, and he can strengthen the outdoor illusion with it by getting mildly sick on his jimmy-pipe.

It is little or no bother. Any man can get hold of enough firewood—say four or five sticks—for a trifle of eight or ten dollars aside from a couple of dollars' taxi fare. He can well have prepared for it months ago anyway.

All kinds of kindly Vermont roadside people sell white-birch sticks three or four inches in diameter for as little as two bits a stick, and it is nothing to bring back a few slivers of that from a fishing trip.

Such makeshift devices do not always satisfy the hardiest outdoorsman, however. I know one who sends to southern Maryland for station-wagon loads of tight-bark hickory, or pignut logs, on the theory that a wood that makes smoked ham taste so good is bound to smell good while burning.

Something went wrong, though, when he tried to smoke a ham in his fireplace with it: he was trying to smoke a smoked ham.

One woman, who lives on Fifth Avenue and used to go deer hunting regularly, has friends from New England bring her back dry apple-tree branches for her fire. She is heavily in debt to the doorman of her apartment house.

These things don't matter much. A man with a fire shining on his face can get more false pleasure into it at the sight of a pair of Christmas boots colored a violent yellow and three sizes too large. The tears forced out by the lovely wood smoke billowing around the living room could easily be tears of joy.

There are added pleasures. For example, yesterday I was at the home of an Ossining man who was preparing for his Christmas fire. He has two fireplaces but can only smoke up one room at a time because both use the same chimney, which was designed for only one.

His firewood, stored in the garage with the lawn mowers and everything else except the car, is building material left over from the time he built the garage.

This man hadn't been hunting for something like a month, and he naturally longed to wear his hunting clothes. The prospective fire enabled him to don leather-faced shooting pants, a twenty-five dollar shooting vest, a red wool cap with fur earflaps, and fifty-dollar waterproof leather boots in order to walk fifteen feet from the kitchen to the garage and carry in an armload of building scraps. He said a hunter needed exercise to keep fit.

The living room smoked up fine with a trial fire. But the big deal will come tomorrow morning. He will be able to open his baby socks with streaming eyes while pulling sickly on one of his eleven jimmy-pipes.

An Outdoorsman Faces
New Year With Many
Resolutions and
Two Cold Feet

Since every self-respecting, red-blooded, right-thinking American hunter and fisherman is bound to make resolutions New Year's Day, the thing might as well be done and cleared away now, and forgotten. Every one of these are going to be kept, too.

Therefore, I virtuously resolve:

To discover or invent some way to keep the feet warm in freezing woods and still be able to walk.

Never again to attempt to ship a bird dog without first consulting Mr. Burke and Mr. Phillips at the Railway Express office in Pennsylvania Station.

To get more trout and bass flies from fly-tying friends by wheedling, whining, threatening, poor-mouthing, blackmailing, and promising.

Not to learn any more fly patterns nor to strain my understanding trying to match them with naturals, with due apology to Ernie Schwiebert, the author of the superb book *Matching the Hatch.*

To remember next fall all of the places where I jumped many grouse while deer hunting with a rifle in my hands.

To take no more than one fall in a stream or lake and a couple in the woods.

Never to drive a car even a hundred yards when I can get somebody else to drive it.

To snarl and use strong, clean language, rather than grin good-naturedly, when companions note I have traveled one hundred miles to fish without bringing a rod. The good-natured grin never satisfies anybody.

173

To hit more quail than Charley Dickey and catch more trout than Dick Wolters, neither of which requires a resolution.

To get some kind of footgear that will keep the feet warm in freezing woods.

To stop carrying too many shells.

Always to carry enough shells.

Not to let anybody convince me that wearing the most visible color is safer in the woods than wearing the least visible color.

To sit still longer than three minutes on a deer stand, and to swear that I sat still for more than three hours.

Never to wash a car or pay to have one washed or get one washed in any other way.

To get some kind of footgear that will keep the feet warm.

Never to fish or hunt with anybody who will want to quit too early.

To keep on saying that fishing contests are intrinsically wrong because they make people fish to beat one another.

To tell the truth at all times about hunting and fishing of any kind anywhere, clarifying it a little sometimes, of course.

To insist that everybody else tell the truth about hunting and fishing, without distorting it under the false guise of clarification.

To discover warm footgear that I can walk in.

Slings and Arrows of Puzzled
Reader Fail to Dent
Milk-Shake-Fortified Hide

Here comes a letter from Walter Gunnison of the Amityville, New York, *Record*. It is a short and seemingly simple letter. But it is not simple; it is full of contemptuous implication. Gunnison could scarcely have written more slander in a book. The entire letter:

> I would like to know what a rod and gun editor does when he is on vacation.
>
> Sincerely,
> Walter Gunnison.

Such grave charges cannot go unanswered forever, although they almost have. Unfortunately they are not new. The A.A.A., or Association of American Actuaries, has officially reckoned that Gunnison's Remark, as it doubtless will come to be known, is made in the form of a question 48,316 times every day of the year.

The Atomic Energy Commission estimates that the energy expended every year in asking the question is sufficient to supply the Commission's Paducah, Kentucky, plant for a week.

No energy has been used in answering it because there is no answer, except bitter silence or a blow. Rod and gun editors have no energy to spare anyway; they are too overworked.

The plain truth is that a rod and gun writer has to spend a good two days of his vacation resting up before he can go hunting or fishing for pleasure. He is exhausted from hunting and fishing for copy and from the physically debilitating influence of milk shakes.

Gunnison and his like never reflect upon, or perhaps do not know about, that grueling milk-shake grind. It is time they did think about it.

Consider that a rod and gun editor goes fishing with Gunnison, or any other angler-for-pleasure. They both get up at 5 A.M., but the reporter is at work and Gunnison is just going fishing.

They fish all day. But Gunnison is just fishing, watching his own fly or plug. The reporter is watching his and Gunnison's, and straining his ears, too. He is afraid Gunnison might say something good, and he has got to get it.

It doesn't matter much whether they catch fish—not to Gunnison, it doesn't. But if they don't, the rod and gun man has to go to one of those places where anglers congregate, and drink milk shakes with them for a couple of hours to get a story.

Then, while Gunnison is still lapping up shakes—or maybe he has switched to strong iced tea by this time—the rod and gun man has to go and write his story. It is then 5 P.M., and he is still at work while Gunnison is listening to lies in the milk bar.

Gunnison could even tell a few lies if he wanted to, although, of course, he doesn't. But the rod and gun man is not even allowed to lie, very much. He is writing current history and must stick rigidly to the truth, sometimes. It is a strain.

But even after he has written his twaddle and had his dinner, the rod and gun man can't relax, or curl up with a good book of comics. He might have missed something good, so he has to drag wearily back to wherever the anglers are congregating, and drink milk shakes with them.

He can't avoid it, either. Gunnison can pass a round, or say his doctor has ordered him off milk shakes, or just say that he has had enough.

But not the rod and gun man. He knows that to refuse an angler's offer of a milk shake will deeply offend that angler. It might even cause the angler on the following day to keep quiet about a notable catch. Of course, that is hardly likely, or even credible, but nobody can know what an insulted angler might do, even if it costs agony.

So the rod and gun man sits there belting one milk shake after another, and cannot stop until the end.

Let Gunnison think about that a little. Gunnison lives no such hard life; he can fish or hunt fecklessly, without thought of the evening, and he can refuse a milk shake whenever he wants to.

There is one other thing the rod and gun man has to do, when he gets back to the office days later, dog-tired from fishing or hunting and writing the truth about them, and shaky from drinking endless milk shakes.

He has to reply to queries such as Gunnison's. It's no job after a vacation, of course. He has done nothing for a while except fish and drink iced tea.